Theological Reflection

Theological Reflection

The Creation of Spiritual Power in the Information Age

Edward O. de Bary

A Michael Glazier Book

LITURGICAL PRESS
Collegeville, Minnesota

www.litpress.org

A Michael Glazier Book published by the Liturgical Press

Cover design by Greg Becker

1   3   5   7   9   8   6   4   2

Library of Congress Cataloging-in-Publication Data
De Bary, Edward O., 1938–
    Theological reflection : the creation of spiritual power in the information age / Edward O. de Bary.
        p. cm.
    "A Michael Glazier book."
    Includes bibliographical references and index.
    ISBN 0-8146-5159-3 (alk. paper)
    1. Theology—Methodology. I. Title.

BR118. D4 2003
230'.01—dc21
                                                            2003044617

Contents

Preface

Beginning a Pilgrimage

At times it seems that one must consider nearly everything under the sun to write about theological reflection. It is about theology to be sure, but it is also about spirituality and ethics. It is about our relationship to God, but it is also about how we relate to one another, and so it involves psychology, sociology, and anthropology. Theological reflection encompasses how we view the world and our understanding of the cosmos, so it also involves cosmology and physics. It is a way of educating, so it is concerned with how we learn and develop. Finally, it is also about how to engage the practice of theological reflection, and so it is about methods. To set all these together is like trying to place a flexible rubber mat on a trampoline with one hand while standing in a large bowl of jelly. When one corner is adjusted, another moves out of place. Meanwhile one's footing shifts because the very ground is unstable. It is challenging, however, because the unexpected is an enduring presence.

To write about theological reflection and place it within these contexts is to encounter the risk of saying much about nothing or saying nothing about many things. At the heart of theological reflection, however, is that longing for the peace of God that surpasses all understanding as we make our pilgrimage through the life that God grants us all.

The Genesis of This Book

For more than twenty-five years I have worked in various positions with the Education for Ministry (EFM),[1] a program whose primary

---

1. The Education for Ministry (EFM) program was developed by Charles L. Winters as an extension program of the School of Theology of the University of

concern is the development of theology and its relationship to the life of faith. Theological reflection is at the heart of that program. Over those years we have explored models and methods of theological reflection so that they could provide the connecting linkage between the experience of the participants in EFM and the biblical and historical traditions of the Christian faith. Early in the development of the program, Charles L. Winters, its founder, recognized that a two-railed fence,[2] first suggested by Ted Ward in 1969, could symbolize the relationship of teaching theology and the ability to "think theologically." He explained the model as a two-railed fence. One rail is the subject under scrutiny—in this case the entire tradition of Christianity, beginning first with the Bible. The other rail is the text each individual brings to the program in the form of his or her life experience. The seminars that engage in theological reflection are the fence posts, the venues for bringing these two together. The heart of the seminar experience is located in the theory and practice of theological reflection. The entire experience, however, is grounded in the supportive community of a small group that worships together. There are two texts: those of the tradition and those of the lives of the participants.

The Purpose

I intend these pages to inform, first of all, for the large community of the Education for Ministry program that works most closely with the methods that I have presented. More broadly, this is intended to suggest to others interested in theology to search for the integration of doing theology with the academic, pastoral, and educational arts.

---

the South, Sewanee, Tennessee in 1975. The four-source model and the methods of theological reflection, which are connected with it, are described in many of its publications. The clearest description may be found in EFM's *Common Lessons and Supporting Materials.* The model originated in the work of Flower Ross who worked with Winters. A description first appeared in academic publications in Patricia O'Connell Killen and John de Beer, "Everyday Theology: A Model for Religious and Theological Education," *Chicago Studies* 22, no. 2 (August 1983). They enlarged on this work in *The Art of Theological Reflection* (New York: Crossroad, 1994). This highly successful program has provided theological education to thousands of laity throughout the world since 1975.

2. Ted Ward, "Programmed Learning Technique Workshop," *Theological Education by Extension,* ed. Ralph D. Winter (South Pasadena, Calif.: William Carey Press, 1969) 321–322.

Theology: An Eclectic Discipline

Frank Whalen, who wrote about the development of the word "theology,"[3] asserts that theology always pertains to God or transcendence and is a second-order activity arising out of faith or spirituality. Theological reflection, as I describe its theory and practice in the chapters that follow, is the establishment of the connection between the first order, the faithful/faithless life, which needs interpretation, and the second order, that of the transcendent interpretation itself. The product of effective theological reflection is a useful transcendent interpretation. But it is also definitively fixed in a life that is meaningful, creative, empowered, and charitable.

Thinking Theologically

Learning to reflect theologically and to think in theological terms involves much more than just the study of theology as an academic pursuit, whether it be biblical, historical, systematic, ethical, pastoral, liturgical, or spiritual. Yet it includes all these. It begins with the conviction that while solitary meditation has a significant role, ultimately the development of theology is a communal affair. Frequently it is best accomplished in small groups or seminars, where participants can develop a process of thinking theologically. The meaning we evolve may be expressed, discussed, checked, enlarged, and integrated. The work of the seminar is intellectual, but it is also emotional, for both affect our decision-making processes and our values. Our theology is systematic inasmuch as it is organized. It is historical and biblical inasmuch as it is rooted in our Christian tradition, the Bible, and our common history. It is pastoral and spiritual inasmuch as it merges from our activities of care and prayer, of Christian action and meditation. In the final analysis, however, our theology is best expressed by our deeds. Our actions are not our salvation, but they certainly declare where our hearts and souls truly repose.

The Structure of This Presentation

The Education for Ministry program, whose work is reflected in this book, developed its own methods and manuals to encourage seminars in the work of theological reflection. Others, of course, have proposed

---

3. Frank Whaling, "The Development of the Word 'Theology,'" *Scottish Journal of Theology* 34, no. 4 (1981) 289–312.

methods for theological reflection that are different. Drawing from the experience of the EFM program, this particular presentation seeks to place the work of theological reflection in a larger context, one that comprises more than methods. Accordingly, the following chapters divide into three parts, followed by an appendix that outlines a series of methods for engaging in theological reflection in a seminar setting or in larger venues.

The first part is an overview that provides some of the theological and historical context for theological reflection. It is not intended to be an exhaustive presentation but rather to lay the groundwork for a theological enterprise as well as to provide a background for the current work. A distinctive emphasis sets this section apart from other works in the field, for it presents theological reflection as an endeavor that belongs to the people of God. (Those inclined to begin learning from practical matters rather than theoretical introductions may prefer to skip Parts I and II and begin with Part III.)

The second part of this book is an introduction to educational theory and methods that apply to the enterprise of theological reflection in a seminar setting. It deals with diverse aspects of the enterprise, from considering how different people learn best in different modalities to how to organize a seminar so that it becomes a learning venue rather than a debating society or a discussion best characterized as ignorance leading ignorance into ennui.

The third part is a presentation of the work of theological reflection—how to organize it, how to direct it, and what needs to be taught to those who desire to direct reflective processes. A theological reflection is an event that is created, guided, and brought to a conclusion. It is more than a glance in the mirror, a chance conversation that turns out to be important, or an unexplainable moment of revelation, although any reflection may have its moments of serendipity. A reflection can be organized. Knowing how to do so has educational implications. While this is aimed at the work of theological reflection, much that is considered in this section can be applied to teaching other disciplines as well.

Finally, a series of appendices outline some specific methods of theological reflection that this writer has used over the years. They are offered with the cautionary note. Leading them, and especially teaching others to lead them, are skills that must be developed. To the uninitiated, manuals are like bathing suits—they usually reveal a great deal, yet the essentials remain hidden, as anyone who has ever tried to learn to work a computer with only a manual and yet did not know where to find the on/off switch can attest. Practice under the supervision of a competent coach is needed to learn how to lead a seminar through the theological reflections that are outlined in the appendices.

Acknowledgments

The work I have produced is the product of centuries of work by other faithful people. I have merely tried to give it shape and present it in an accessible manner and added a few ideas of my own. To be sure, there are some people who deserve special mention. Charles L. Winters founded the Education for Ministry program as a program in theological education by extension. A former student of Paul Tillich, this shows in his concept of the possibility of thinking theologically. His wife Flower Ross developed the initial methods for EFM and made an immense contribution both in methods and training. Her successor in that work, John de Beer, and some of our colleagues, especially Richard E. Brewer, Paul Dyer, George Gerl, Robert Hughes, Gail Jones, Patricia O'Connell Killen, Elizabeth Lang, Carolyn Kinman Lankford, Trevor Smith, and Liz Workman, developed models and methods for theological reflection that continue to produce fruitful results. But they did not do this alone. The Education for Ministry team of trainers who reside in the United States, England, Canada, Australia, the Bahamas, and New Zealand have produced many pieces of the total work. In turn, they are in debt to the thousands of EFM mentors and most especially the EFM students, who have shared their insights, comments, and suggestions over a period of nearly thirty years.

Finally, I must thank those who have worked closely with me to help produce these pages. Special thanks to to those who have assisted in the production of materials for the Education for Ministry program. These include Deborah Shrum, Priscilla Fort, and Cynthia Hargis. Productive collaboration with Dr. Thomas A. Huff, M.D., of the Medical College of Georgia helped to produce the pages on the various levels of discourse. My niece Laura Hileman Huff gave these pages an early editorial perusal and provided many valuable suggestions. At the Liturgical Press I thank especially the editors who have collaborated to produce this work, John Schneider, Jr., and Colleen Stiller. My wife Marcia has been a loving and supportive colleague and critic through all the years during which these ideas developed. Without her this would not have been possible. Finally I remember most gratefully our parents who supported and loved us and now observe what we do from the point of view of the greater life: T. Marx and Gladys Allen Huff and Edmond T. and Annemarie Merton de Bary.

Edward Oscar de Bary
Sewanee, Tennessee
March 1, 2003

PART I

Theological Reflection
Historical, Philosophical, and Theological Context

The reader may prefer to read first about concrete expressions of theological reflection. If so, he or she may wish to read Part III and the Appendices first. Then, Parts I and II may be read in that order to put the reality in context.

CHAPTER 1

Theological Reflection
What It Is and Why

A Complex Endeavor

Reflection is a basic building block of any educational or learning process. Something happens in which we are involved. We describe or examine our experience of that event. We ponder and think about it as well as use the resources we possess to illuminate our understanding. We draw conclusions and we establish the basis for future actions. Should we refuse to reflect, we deny ourselves the opportunity to learn, to adapt, and to grow. A failure to reflect leads to the eternal repetition of the same mistakes again and again. It enacts the myth of Sisyphus, who repeatedly rolls a stone up a hill only to have it roll back down. His destiny prevents him from reflecting on his actions, and so he never learns how to block the stone and keep it from falling back to its original position.

To describe the tasks involved in theological reflection is fairly easy. It is also easy to write a process or checklist for how to lead a theological reflection; however, a reflective activity is a means rather than an end in itself. It has a purpose, and that purpose is set within a context that makes the entire endeavor complex as well as interesting and engaging.

The capacity to reflect is directly related to our capacity to discover and learn. Our knowledge about ourselves and the world depends on reflection, taking the opportunity to acquire information, ponder it, set it into meaningful relationships, and then make use of the conclusions. This is a continuous process, cyclical, but also extended into time. It is less like a wheel spinning than like a wheel rolling down a road, thereby acquiring and discarding as it travels. Because change occurs as the process of reflection proceeds, it is a double-edged sword. Unfortunately, the same reflective processes can tend to cause participants to discard what is useful and acquire destructive tendencies, even while they learn what is instructive, productive, and creative. Thus an important aspect of teaching theological reflection is to prepare a context, a venue, and a process for reflection that emphasizes what is constructive and allows participants to avert results that cause harm, destruction, or needless suffering.

A reflective process is also itself a learning process. Writing about theological reflection as a process of discovering and learning about our faith is to consider the merits of an educational process. This means that as we examine the role of theological reflection, we must consider educational methods and needs. People appropriate and organize what they learn in different ways; consequently, a discussion of theological reflection as an educational tool must also consider learning styles and educational methodology.

Ancient Roots

The need to reflect, if we are not to be caught in a vicious cycle, is not a new insight. The ancient Greeks knew well that "the unexamined life is not worth living." According to Plato (420–347 B.C.E.), who quoted Socrates (469–399 B.C.E.),[1] "Know yourself!" was the motto of the oracle at Delphi. The process of reflection described above can be reduced to four simple steps: (1) action [do]; (2) identify the key elements [look]; (3) analyze the information [think]; and (4) generalize for the future [plan]. Yet it is a complex endeavor. It is especially complicated when applied to the domain of theology, which strives to bring meaning to life. Only when life has meaning, of course, do we truly develop the power to be creative human beings made in the image of God.

Unfortunately, Plato's philosophy suggests that one should begin the reflective process with a theory or philosophy. He thought that this mental phase is more truly real than their concrete expressions in the world. The everyday world is perishable, while ideas are eternal. For Plato,

---

1. Plato, *The Apology*. Plato wrote a dialogue that recorded a conversation between Socrates and his students. These were Socrates' final words, uttered as he prepared to drink a cup of hemlock and die. He advocated the value of reflection or philosophical thinking. Today, asking open-ended or reflective questions is sometimes called the "Socratic method." Another term for it is the "maieutic" method, which refers to the process of giving birth.

the ideas or the forms they depict are the reality of which all the "things" of the world are only imperfect and, therefore, temporary copies.

Plato's student, the Greek philosopher Aristotle (384–322 B.C.E.), followed a different path, one of analysis and investigation. He also subsumed theology, mathematics, and physics under the topic of philosophy. While his works did not dominate the development of theology until the Middle Ages, when the philosophy of Plato became less important to Western theologians, Aristotle's influence today remains very strong. For him, theology includes metaphysics as well as a doctrine of divine nature. His thinking helped to usher in the Renaissance and the age of science and technology, which now dominates our lives. Since Aristotle subsumed theology to philosophy, the long-term effect tended to reduce theology and remove it from the marketplace of life.

To be sure, Aristotle's philosophy was not the only new factor. As the early churches developed during the first five centuries of the Christian era, theology became the property of the religious communities or the Church, thereby escaping the clutches of pagan philosophy. At the base of theology, of course, was the faith of the Church and its people, rooted in the Bible. By the Middle Ages, Thomas Aquinas set forth the notion that theology involves knowledge of reality, in a word, the totality of all that is, a science that is the "queen of the sciences." While Thomas Aquinas related theology to nature, he nevertheless also placed the former in an esoteric and exalted position. For Thomas, theology and philosophy are contiguous disciplines. Thus he combined philosophy and the biblical heritage into a reflective edifice sometimes known as the "Medieval Synthesis."

What Is Theological Reflection?

Vox populi vox dei—"The voice of the people is the voice of God," for God speaks through creation, and the human experience is our most direct contact with that divine voice. It comes especially (but not only) to the people of God, that communion of saints we call the Church (the Church in the widest sense, not a particular group or denomination). Perhaps it also extends across religious lines and encompasses all the traditions that emerged from the biblical traditions that tell of Abraham and Sarah. Learning to think theologically offers something different from slavish or literal affirmations of faith. It does not permit a separation of faith and the remainder of our lives, nor does it allow for a denial of all religion. Thinking theologically means looking at the richness of the human experience to discover its meaning by recognizing the transcendent factors that connect us to one another and to the divine milieu.

To write about theological reflection in this way invites everyone to participate in that process. There exists, of course, for our purpose, a particularly Christian point of view to consider. God speaks to Christians through the Body of Christ, the Church, as well as through Holy Scripture. We do not limit God's existence to the Church, but we know that, at the very least, God may be found there. Those who wish to know Jesus find God through what God provided—the Church, the *ecclesia*, the assembly of all baptized people, the communion of saints.

The Role of Specialists

To be sure, the Church has long supported a cadre of specialists who attend to the theological needs of the community. The academicians and clerics have their special and necessary roles to keep us intellectually honest and press the processes of adaptation and discovery. They are often best positioned to assist the people of God cope with the demands of scientific discoveries and technology that turn our assumptions upside down. Church leadership, bishops, presidents, moderators, and clerics have their special responsibilities as formal guardians and teachers of the Church's teachings. Clergy or ordained persons direct liturgical functions and may offer counsel. But ultimately the ministry and theology of the Church belong to all its members, and therefore effective ministers are also effective theologians. Since the ministry is a shared function, theology belongs to God's people. It is the voice of the people. The specialists and the clerics have their role, but the people of God, the communion of saints past and present, are the final arbiters of the Church's theology when it is expressed in human terms.

Why Muse About Theological Reflection?

What does it mean to "reflect theologically"? Is there such a thing as "thinking theologically"? Why should we claim to engage in theological reflection and thought other than as an academic enterprise? Perhaps this challenge is disturbing. To endeavor to "think theologically" may be something new to the reader. Yet theology touches all human enterprises at some point, because it is ultimately a search for meaning. The word "meaning" conveys the notion of intellectual understanding, but in this context it is much more. It includes possessing or discovering that sense of life that expresses our reason for living, that basic energy that moves us and is at the core of our being. For that reason this book ranges across a diverse group of subjects. The Latin word *religo,* meaning "to tie fast," from which we derive the word "religion," conveys the linkage that religions provide. Theology is the discipline of thinking about linkages, ultimate linkages, the search for meaning and purpose, the religious and divine connection.

When we develop our theology and find what gives meaning to our lives, we discover that decisions follow our insights. These are the implications of our discoveries. The discovery of faith is not an end in itself. Christian action is the effective application of what we learn. The result is that our own theological reflection as well as the decision to lead others to "think theologically" involves an ethical component that is not to be ignored. To ignore what we learn is as much a moral (perhaps immoral or amoral, depending on the wisdom of the choice) action as a decision to pursue a particular course. All this is part and parcel of the enterprise of theological thinking into which the reader is invited to join, not as an observer, but as a lifelong participant.

Pastoral Theology

A most basic aspect of any theology is its pastoral dimension. It involves bringing theological meaning where nonsense seems to exist—to the hurts, needs, and anguish of the people of God. Being a pastor means bringing reconciliation where alienation thrives and creating opportunities for celebration when occasions for joy erupt. Pastoral theology provides the rationale for the meaning of the sacramental functions that celebrate the great transitions of life—birth, maturation, marriage, vocation, and death.

The pastoral task is very personal, but it is also communal. Ultimately, theology that fails its pastoral obligations to express God's love is a failed theology. Thus the pastoral criteria are the ultimate test to assay the orthodoxy of every theological proposition. They are better indicators of theological validity than the biblical and doctrinal test that some prefer to apply. Indeed, I contend that the pastoral test trumps all others.[2]

Thus, for example, Old Testament admonitions against the use of blood are sound in the historical context of the Old Testament and the

---

2. No less than Karl Rahner argues that the critical conscience of the theological disciplines is found in practical theology, for he suggests that the very basis for practical theology is its pastoral application. Karl Rahner, *Confrontations I,* Theological Investigations 11 (New York: Seabury Press, 1974).

threat of diseases that the blood might spread. Today, with our knowledge of medicine, however, it makes no sense to use such admonitions to justify the denial of a life-saving transfusion or of transplanting organs, as some Christian groups still believe. Moreover, I suggest that using biblical or doctrinal precepts as a pretext to avoid difficult pastoral considerations is *per se* a sinful and destructive activity.

There are at least two justifications for my condemnation of that kind of legalism. First, it avoids accepting responsibility. Second, it denies the pastoral concern that is the basis for the very existence of Holy Scripture and doctrinal stipulations, namely, God's love for all that God has created. When these considerations apply to controversial topics pertaining to moral choices about life, death, and sexuality, the theological reflections become both important and weighty, for they provide a methodology to engage life's most important decisions. These decisions are not to be reserved for high councils and synods alone. They impinge on everyone at some time or another, such as when attending a family member or friend *in extremis*. Decisions of gravity require careful consideration. Making such decisions always includes a theological reflection because our fundamental values are at stake.

The Search for Transcendence

Yet there is more. Theological reflection also involves something beyond the personal and the pastoral. Being the pastor may be where the rubber of theology hits the road of life, but the writings of theologians also lead elsewhere. Leading one through the ups and downs of life as a "good shepherd" is a noble and vital venture, but theology is more than a personal coping with life's events. Theology also contains the search for relationship that provides transcendent connections. More important, well-honed theological thinking can provide meaning to what appears to be tragic and senseless. For that reason, the ability to think theologically also brings hope when there is despair. Just where and how to find the basis for meaning is at the crux of the theological enterprise.

Theology: Absolute or Relative?

Again and again, in various ways, the world has observed and participated, sometimes to the point of war, in debates between those who affirm that theology is constructed on great absolutes and those who take a position that all that we know is merely relative. Those who focus on the absolute(s) offer a very constrained view of reality. That constriction may feel like shackles to those who differ with them. To those who believe in absolutes, others appear to exist in a relativistic bath, an outlook that seems amoral and without foundation or basis. Again and again absolutism and relativism inevitably lead to tension and conflicts. Morally, neither offers genuine assistance.

Learning to think theologically is an attempt to provide ways to move beyond positions that only provide dead ends and discords that are inevitable when we take positions from which we cannot budge. Theological thinking must be flexible in order to adapt to an ever changing reality and to the steadfast love of God. A coherent sense of our own theology must be neither trapped in absolute demands nor flabby because of a cynical relativism. We need to find another path. Many have struggled with this in the past. Perhaps this is one way of understanding the meaning and importance of Jacob's struggle in the night at Peniel that led to his new name and a displaced hip (Gen 32:24ff.) The answer, I suggest, is to develop a theology that is relational.

A Relational Theology: The Model of the Diamond

Thomas Aquinas's theological summary combined a theology from above with a theology from below (although he never wrote of it precisely in that way) by suggesting that the universe is circular. He also combined Christianity with the philosophies of Plato and Aristotle. Aquinas's theology sought to be at once transcendent and imminent. All begins with God, passes through the world, and returns to God. Thus Aquinas incorporated Greek philosophy into his theological schema. But the circle was linear, in that one thing always led to another, and it was hierarchical, with God at the pinnacle. This synthesis, as elegant as it was, did not last, and it no longer serves us well today, although the point of view it represents is still very much alive.

A NONLINEAR MODEL WITH FOCUS

To point to the transcendental relationships for which we must account—our human frailties and the presence of God in our lives—I propose the metaphor of a diamond. With it, I think we can delineate a relational model and our limited place in the vastness of creation. We can also perceive the divine presence that brings us into relationship with all that exists.

To begin, imagine a cut diamond that a jeweler has prepared for a setting. It has the shape of a cone and lacks any curves. The cut lines clearly delineate every facet that appears on the part that will be visible, the part we admire. Light enters the diamond through its facets at the top of the stone and travels to the tip of the cone, from which it reflects back to the face of entry and out of the stone toward our eyes. What we admire is the reflection of the light sparkling from the many facets on the surface of the diamond. Each facet lies in a slightly different plane, so that the light comes from multiple angles. This gives the diamond its glittering appearance. The light seems to shimmer when there is move- ment. Yet each facet offers a path to the very tip of the diamond. The light reflects from the very same point, the tip of the diamond, regard- less of the facet by which it enters or exits. All we see is reflected light.

Imagine next that each facet is analogous to the lenses through which we peer at an event. Each facet represents a point of view or per- spective. These lenses may be those of the professional or the amateur. They may belong to the chemist or the physicist, the housewife or the student, the pastor or the physician, the practitioner of voodoo or the politician, the sociologist or the anthropologist. The tip of the diamond is analogous to any event upon which we may fix our gaze. Each of us views the reality of the event through the facet or lens particular to our point of view, knowledge, discipline, as well as through our own distor- tions and prejudices.

Following another analogy, one described by the physicist Sir Arthur Eddington, the lenses of the diamond work like a net. The char- acteristics of the fish that are snared depend upon the size and character of the mesh that makes up the net. In the model of the diamond, the lenses represent the characteristics that determine what the world or a particular event looks like from a particular point of view.[3] Our human limitations restrict us to a particular time and place; consequently, we can only look at reality through one particular lens or point of view at a time. Although we may possess the ability to look at other aspects of an event, the information we receive at any particular moment is always limited to one point of view. Any other information we have while we study a par- ticular perspective becomes available as a function of our memory and the projections of our imagination. This poses certain problems.

---

3. The analogy of the fish net was employed by the physicist G. J. Whitrow, *The Structure of the Universe* (London: Hutchinson, 1946), 151, who ascribed it to Sir Arthur Eddington. It was adopted by Eric L. Mascall, *Christian Theology and Natural Science* (London: Longmans Green, and Co., 1956) 113.

Sociologist Robert W. Friedrichs presents an aspect of the problem that occurs because our cognitive ability is subjective and restricted, as the model of the diamond suggests. He states that there are competing frames of reference, which exist in paradox or juxtaposition, much like the facets of the diamond.

> The key that would unlock the paradox is the recognition that the competing frames are not simply alternative but nested as well. The eyes we all have—scientists and non-scientists alike—register experiences that cluster about the complementary poles of the intrasubjective and the intersubjective, the unique and the recurrent, the existential and the relational. Given a preference for efficient prediction some— eventually all at times—will use a polarized lens to filter out the first of each pair and focus simply upon the second, projecting order over time in the manner of science.[4]

Friedrich's statement is difficult to follow because the paradox to which he points is complex. A polarized lens cuts out unnecessary light or information. His metaphor of a polarized lens is a way of narrowing the area to be surveyed so that the information can be analyzed. Friedrichs offers a way of observing more than one frame of reference simultaneously. This is a way to cope with the fact that human beings generally can only do one of two things at the same time. We may observe an event and study its details as something hypothetically static, or we may look at the development or motion of the event. Neither can be done simultaneously. When taking a photograph of a galloping horse, either the horse or the background will be blurred. Which will appear blurred depends upon whether we select to follow the motion of the horse or focus on the background. Both cannot be examined simultaneously by a single observation with clarity. When we take multiple observations, we use our imagination to develop their relationship, so that the sum of two or more observations can reveal more than each part.

In our minds, however, we can relate the static with the mobile, or even two or more movements in multiple dimensions. We can also connect information from different points of view, but to do this we must communicate or bring our disparate opinions into relationship. To make that linkage, we need the benefit of memory as well as communication.

4. Robert W. Friedrichs, *A Sociology of Sociology* (New York: The Free Press, 1970) 298–299.

Without them we are unable to make sense of our experiences. In theology this kind of recollection has long been known, especially in liturgical forms, as anamnesis[5] (a calling up in a new way), exactly the opposite of amnesia (forgetting).

To establish communications between individuals who share closely linked points of view is relatively easy. They share common borders. For example, the physician can communicate relatively easily with the biologist or the chemist.[6] But when the viewpoints are from widely disparate origins, the communications are much more tenuous. At times they may be virtually impossible until some common line of interest or demarcation is identified. For instance, someone who pursues voodoo as a means of treating those who are ill may find it difficult to communicate with a psychiatrist or a surgeon about professional matters. They may both observe the same sick person, but their interpretation and their reaction or treatment will be very different. Yet if persons who represent different points of view are to search for meaning, they must search for links that join together varying points of view in some way or another. They must seek a common language, links, and relationships.

The search for linkage is fundamentally a theological task. It is a step in the search for the meaning of life. As such, it ultimately leads to the transcendent and the discovery of the divine that connects us to the universe. It represents a theological quest that is at once rooted in human experience and discovered in the majestic wonders of creation. Those who engage in this search as their profession are theologians, and those who do this from a Christian context are Christian theologians. But everyone must do this, at least to some degree; otherwise life becomes only a limited and unorganized series of events that terminate in

5. This Greek term is sometimes poorly translated as a recalling and memorializing that conjure a sense of either bringing back the past or commemorating it. Actually, *anamnesis* is better understood as a calling to mind or a lively reminiscence. There is a firm linkage to the past, but there is also something new and unique with each act we label as anamnesis. Perhaps it is more closely related to our notion of a "flashback," a moment of recall that is real, powerful, and alive rather than a reference to a mere recollection or memory. It may also be understood as calling the past into communion with the present so that we may extend that linkage into the future. That is what we celebrate when we say that we belong to "the communion of saints."

6. The analogy of the lenses also applies to persons with similar professions or points of view. Our lenses are always shaped or colored by our education, experience, personal preferences, and a host of cultural and genetic factors.

death. Thus, to be a theologian is a fundamental task in which we all engage in some way, unless we prefer the suicide of a lonely cynic.

Theology and Dialectics

Our theology has consequences. It forms our values, identifies what is important, and predicts what we will reject or ignore. In no way should the theological task be oversimplified to a series of propositions or a synthesis of religious expressions. Theology is more than simply linking points of view, and it is more than a movement from one proposition to its negation in order to evolve a synthesis—a process commonly called "dialectics" by philosophers. Although dialectics may provide a useful tool that can clarify, amalgamate, synthesize, or distinguish various relationships, and thus be a useful aspect of the theological enterprise, it remains just that—a tool. It is not itself a theological endeavor. But dialectics does involve a fundamental problem that frequently occurs in theology, namely, how to achieve unity amidst diversity. Dialectics is fundamentally dualism or binary opposition seeking unification; it can take theology down a dualistic path. Theology can use dialectics as a device to enable discernment, but the theological task is to relate the whole cosmos rather than to engage in a process of synthesizing, a debate or contest.[7]

The theologian must move further than simply reconciling two points of view, because a second point of view may only add an illusion of depth. The theologian has the task of reaching ever further afield, linking myriad points and levels of view, so that connections with what appears to be unrelated and disconnected emerge. To achieve a set of images or ideas that enables us to paint a holistic picture requires something more than rational expressions. In addition to theories and philosophies, the imagery of myths and metaphors, visions, and dreams

---

7. This discussion may remind some readers of Edward Farley, *Theologia: The Fragmentation and Unity of Theological Education* (Philadelphia: Fortress Press, 1983). Farley was striving to recover a sense of *theologia* from the academic world that tends to break down the subject into its component parts. He wanted to recover for theology the ". . . personal, sapiential knowledge (understanding) which can occur when faith opens itself to reflection and inquiry" (p. 156). This is very much the kind of process I am trying to describe in these pages, especially in the Part III and in the Appendices. Where I differ with Farley is in the location of the primary venue for this kind of endeavor. Farley would place it in *academia;* I would place it in the *ecclesia.* Farley would concentrate on scholarship; I would concentrate on the voice of the people of God, inclusive of academics, of course.

are important tools to establish the linkage that holds together our perceptions of the universe. In his Bampton Lectures of 1948, Austin Farrar proposed that the inspiration nascent in revelation emerges through images that make supernatural revelation possible. Thus it has been maintained: "Religious truth can be expressed more adequately under the forms of imagination—symbol, image, myth, drama, parable, liturgical rite and sacramental action—than in the propositions of the intellect."[8]

Thus the task of the theologian is to give sense to the meaning of history through the bridge of our imagination, a reminder of Edward Schillebeeckx's observation that the theologian is the "shepherd of transcendence."[9] The theologian brings meaning to life by looking retrospectively at history and prospectively toward the eschatological promise of the future. By linking the gaps between various events, the theologian brings meaning to the apparent chaos of existence. The experience transforms and helps us to reach beyond the mundane. In the words of Thomas F. Torrance, "In theological thinking we have to break through the surface to the depths of intelligible reality and engage with orderly relations lodged in it that reach far beyond our experience and understanding."[10]

We all cope with the questions of meaning in our lives, and so we are all called to be theologians. We are all called to be shepherds of transcendence.

8. Alan Richardson, "The Rise of Modern Biblical Scholarship and Recent Discussion of the Authority of the Bible," *The Cambridge History of the Bible,* ed. S. L. Greensdale (Cambridge: The University Press, rept. 1976) 334. Richardson cites Austin Farrar, *The Glass of Vision* (London, 1948), lecture 3.

9. Edward Schillebeeckx, *Geloofverstaan: Interpretatie en Krietiek* (Bloemendaal: Nelissen, 1972) 186.

10. Thomas F. Torrance, *Theological Science* (London: Oxford University Press, 1969) 129.

CHAPTER 2

The Work of Theological Reflection
Background

The Historical Basis for Doing Theology

Many hold the perception that Christian theology is an intellectual pursuit that academics pursue. It is biblical and follows a reasonable and rational line that can only be articulated by those who have studied the history and philosophy that provide theology with its intellectual framework. For some, theology is the articulation of faith in God in philosophical terms; for others, it is the intellectualization of faith. This conundrum has been the fodder of debates that go back more than a millennium. Where does theology begin—with faith or with reason? Anselm of Canterbury, during the tenth century, suggested that understanding emerged from faith. By the end of the Middle Ages, a new understanding of science was on the horizon, and those who searched for scientific advances (like Roger Bacon in the thirteenth century) suggested that we investigate with reason in order that we might discover faith. Anselm's famous phrase was reversed. He had said, "I believe in order that I might have understanding" (faith seeking reason or understanding). The new view said, "I seek understanding in order that I might have faith" (reason seeking to discover faith).

At its high point in the Middle Ages, theology combined the Christian heritage and the philosophical disciplines with the brilliance of imaginative thinking. When universities first developed, scientists did not clearly separate imagery and scientific rigor. They did not employ the laboratory method of discovery, establishing hypotheses and testing for veracity. For example, astrology and astronomy were one discipline, as were chemistry and alchemy. Philosophy and theology were grouped under one umbrella, and at the time they also included between them what later came to be known as psychology. The primacy of faith and theology, however, frequently led to obfuscation and a reluctance to accept the consequences of scientific discoveries that might render faithful assumptions obsolete.

With the rise of scientific methods, scientists noticed that religious imagery was often a subterfuge for ignorance, prejudice, and a lack of discipline. They began to emphasize rational thinking through disciplined observations, experimental science, and deductive conclusions that could be proved by repeatable demonstrations. The insights of imagery, dreams, fantasy, and artistic expressions became suspect except as objects of analytical study. The natural sciences and the arts grew apart. As a result, academic theology reduced its exploration of imagery and insisted on scientific proofs, or at least rationalized arguments acceptable to philosophers. It became the discipline of religious studies, while theology remained in seminaries and monasteries. Academics tended to relegate the mysterious aspects of faith to the darker corners of acceptability. Spirituality, religious fervor, and academic rigor could not coexist easily, because an academic stance required a certain distance from the subject under scrutiny.

This alienation continues today, when we experience the conflict between the apparent rationality of academia and the fervor of charismatic movements. They are often at odds and, at the very least, remain suspicious of each other. Today one still hears arguments that derive from the ancient debate between faith and reason, but the scenario has changed. Often the divergence occurs between the proponents of emotional enthusiasm as a sign of faithful belief and those who provide a philosophical analysis to explain the core of the theological enterprise.

As the age of science and technology developed, theology continued to suffer. It could not be forced into the rigor of scientific analysis according to the rules of the laboratory. No matter what kind of philosophical background existed, theology tended to become a historical theology or a linguistic analysis—very dry subjects for those in the pews. As a result, theology slowly receded from its important position in the academic curriculum, until departments of religion became nearly totally divorced from the practices of faith. In the meantime, the religion of the people in the pews became separated from the speculations of theologians. Popular and charismatic speakers held out for the "old time religion" and rejected scientific discoveries. While they were well known, they were not the leading scholars.

The Rise of Religious Studies

To relate better to the academic community, theology during the twentieth century tended to become a formal and rational discipline known as "religious studies." Students of religion could be nonbelievers seeking to study religion objectively, an anomaly when compared with other disciplines. How could someone who did not believe in the efficacy of medicine become a physician or one who did not believe in the importance of the rule of law become an attorney? The effect was to treat religion as an object rather than as a lively activity shared by all, like the air we breathe.

The creative aspects or nonrational activities either ended, were turned over to the artists, were left to the unsophisticated pious believers, or were seized by the con artists who used religion as theater to create political arenas from which to gain power and wealth. Literary works rather than religious expressions often became primary forms for poignant metaphorical expressions of faith. Beginning with the sixteenth century, a brilliant era in literature arose, but as time passed, it contained less and less that both religion and the Church could sponsor. The authors of novels, short stories, dramas, and poetry often dealt with the great theological themes, but they did so at the risk of ecclesiastical condemnation. Their works were not considered to be "theological," because they failed to appear to be sufficiently pious.

Today many theologians see the theological value of the secular arts. Nevertheless, the risks still remain, especially in portions of the world dominated by repressive religious regimes, that pious conservatives will regard such works as an affront to faith. We may see this more clearly today in the Moslem world when ancient works of art are destroyed in the name of piety, but Christianity has also known its periods of iconoclasm, so we should not be too smug or self-righteous. The same forces exist among Christians.

As we begin the twenty-first century, the supporters of scientific rationalism have generally won the day in the universities but not in the popular expressions of faith found in the religious establishments. Today most people think that theology is an academic discipline that requires a long preparation. What they seek is different. They desire caring pastors who may be trusted. They care for inspiring leadership that brings out the best of the community. And they hope for a future with meaning and value.

The Appeal of That "Old Time Religion"

Many who attend church services regularly also emphasize faith rather than reason when they think of religion. They honor the past and yearn for a return to the "golden days," which may have never existed. To balance this with modernity, they frequently separate faith from other aspects of their lives. For them, the scientific contributions to theological thinking have merit, but thinking theologically needs to go beyond a scholarly approach. It also needs to go beyond the academic or priestly professional because it must provide a vision of faith that remains faithful to the past. Those who treasure the past should not be ignored, because they remind us that God has always spoken through the people, those present, past, and future. We cannot and should not return to the past, but we ignore it at our peril. Theology ultimately belongs to all God's people. Whether we like it or not, whether we do it well or not—like breathing—all of us engage in theological thinking if we are alive and conscious. This means that we must take seriously a conservative critique lest we lose the valuable lessons of the past. A serious consideration, however, is quite different from uncritical adoption. Much of what passes for conservatism is really unfortunate and uninformed pap, while much that passes for liberalism is a momentary response that fails to account for current sensibilities or the rich legacy of the past.

Theology for the People of God

What, then, is theology if we entertain a populist notion of its scope? Theology is an art form as well as a rational intellectual process. We lose our moorings when we fail to include the mind, the body, and the heart in our theological enterprises. The role of the theologian is to integrate our self-understanding, our universe, and the presence of God so that our lives have meaning and congruence. This means that all our abilities—to reason, to create, to analyze, to act, to be artists, scientists and engineers—must be engaged to reflect on theology's proper domain. That domain encompasses all life's activities as well as something beyond us, something divine that transcends our human frailties.

Now all this brings us to a critical point, recognizing that a theological study cannot be independent of its own subject matter. No less than Thomas Torrance has pointed out that we have come to a point where it is not possible to separate the way in which we know from the actual knowledge we possess.[1] Yet both how we know God and what we

1. Thomas F. Torrance, *Theological Science* (London: Oxford University Press, 1969) 10ff.

know about God are at stake in theological reflection. The art of reflecting theologically is the art of dealing with this issue. It comes out of the recognition that our theology comes from multiple places and emerges in the dialogue between the world, our sources of authority, our community, and ourselves.

Thinking About God

The word "theology" literally means "the study of God." This title for a scientific enterprise seems incongruous. We presume the truth of the Scripture that says, "No one has ever seen God,"[2] yet we presume to have a discipline that would study the divine. How arrogant!

History brings to us the work of a multitude of thoughtful Christian theologians. They all sought to grapple with the existence and meaning of God and to understand God's grace in a fallen world. They agonized over the evil that falls upon the innocent and the guilty, and they stumbled over the difficulties we still experience today. They developed arguments to demonstrate the existence of God and developed lengthy and complicated proofs for their arguments. They also sought to describe God or at least the divine attributes. Those who were sufficiently thoughtful knew that the attempts to approach the divine through philosophy were useful but also that they were limited.

Theology Today

Some theologians know that the classical descriptions of divine attributes are insufficient analogies. They are also unable to create metaphorical images that truly describe the divine. They know that the psalmist is right when he proclaims that only a fool claims to have seen God.[3] The reality of God is beyond any description or imagery that can be conceived by human beings. These theologians believe that God is beyond us as well as immanent. Even restricting theology to analogy and metaphor can deceive and lead us to believing that God is in the image of humanity rather than the other way around. The temptation of idolatry is much more profound and much more common than simply worshiping idols.

Thinking About the Universe

Theology frequently begins with our understanding or doctrine of God or our doctrine of humanity. It begins with the story of the Fall of

2. John 1:18.
3. Psalm 14:1.

Adam in the Garden of Eden, which is told in the Book of Genesis. This focuses on where human beings live and how humanity relates to God. There is prior action, however, and the focus on humanity leads to a larger framework. The Bible begins with the story of creation. God, apart from the cosmos, is not a divinity we know. Our experience is always mediated by our existence with, in, and as part of the universe. Thus theologians as well as faithful believers have long contemplated the meaning of the universe as a pathway to understanding divine activity. God appears to be limited by the creation only because we are inseparable from it. If there is no creation of the cosmos, there is also no creation of humanity, so for human beings God does not exist apart from the universe we inhabit.

Thinking about the universe—observing the movement of the objects we see in the sky, contemplating the meaning of time and space, and dealing with the structures of matter and causation—all these are part of the theological task. Many think this to be esoteric, that it requires special scientific and philosophical knowledge, yet everyone has a way of understanding the universe. Whether God does or does not fit into that comprehensive model depends upon our perspective rather than upon a sophisticated knowledge; therefore, even if only at the elementary level, we are all physicists, chemists, biologists, philosophers, and also theologians. We decide for our purposes our relationship to the cosmos, and we infer meaning to our existence through this description.

Our understanding of cosmology has changed over the two millennia that Christianity has dominated the Western world. When astronomy could no longer describe the cosmos as a flat earth with God safely in the heavens, thought to exist beyond the realm of the moon, sun, and stars, a major crisis for science, for common sense, and for theology occurred. The new cosmic model of the solar system was frightening to the average person and theologian alike, for both thought that the world was flat and that the sun rotated around the earth, pointing to the center of God's creation, the earth. The thought that the earth might be round and that it rotated around the sun suggested that someone might fall off the bottom side. More alarming, humanity was no longer the center of the universe. When we discovered that the earth and the planets twirl around the sun rather than vice-versa, we discovered that our vast world is an "island home," just a small planet spinning around a minor star located in a remote arm of a mediocre galaxy. In its self-image and cosmological descriptions, humanity no longer occupied a privileged position as the centerpiece of God's creative activity. Worse, it was not even possible to identify the centerpiece.

In the twentieth century a new cosmological model developed, and the heliocentric model that grew during the Renaissance was challenged. Just as Nicolai Copernicus, Galileo Galilei, and the physics of Isaac Newton once challenged the earlier Ptolemaic cosmology, which argued for a flat earth at the center of all creation, we now believe that even time and space, as well as matter and energy, are not absolutes. We have found the universe to be even more complicated and marvelous. But in the cosmic physical picture, God no longer has a safe heaven to which all pure souls rise. Nor is God at some cosmic core. From a human perspective, which is the only one we can establish, the new physics do not allow the divine to be outside the universe, because the very boundaries of the universe are unknown. All we can know is within the limits of our vision (knowability), and these limits continually change. We can appropriate and clarify our reality, but this is always a subjective view, not an objective knowledge.[4] That fundamental factor dominates all theological reflection as we know it at present.

We can no longer successfully perceive ourselves to be at the center of the universe, as theologians suggested during the Middle Ages. Nor can we posit a circular and mechanistic system that possesses a divine perfection. Science now suggests that there is certain absurdness that characterizes the creation. Our immediate experience of the universe is that we live in a box that represents an enclosed system. Our perception of the box is that it possesses its proper characteristics, for we perceive its sides or limits and we can measure how far we are from its boundaries. But it is a peculiar box. Regardless of how fast we move or in what direction we travel, we find that we are always at the same distance from every side of the container, for the sides represent the limits of our perception. It is a box with sides but without limits, yet the paradox exists that we are limited within it. Our limits permit us to perceive only our boundaries, what I would call the "event horizon." If we had not become aware of this phenomenon, we would always presume that we are at the center, because our primary senses would tell us this and no more. What the new physics has achieved is to allow human beings to transcend their limited senses and make use of that knowledge. That is what computers and all the electronic apparatus of the twenty-first century are really about.

4. Bernard J. F. Lonergan, *Method in Theology* (New York: Seabury Press, 1972) 262.

The recognition that we are at once at the center and also on the edge, without final reference as to where we truly are, has produced a crisis for theology, but it is also a crisis for the average Christian—where do we find God? Can we cope with the notion of God who is everywhere and also nowhere? The answer, of course, is yes, just as we accept that God is both personal and transcendent. The meaning of all this, however, is difficult to express. In matters theological and their derivative in moral theology, it seems that we no longer have boundaries. We can try to "draw lines in the sand," but it is just that—a momentary line drawn in a shifting matrix. Only an adequate reflection can lead us out of the morass that some try to avoid with rigid formulas and incantations.

Part of the difficulties we encounter in theology is that our interpretation of our relation to the universe, our doctrine of creation, has yet to catch up with the new science that continues to emerge. Simply putting God before the big bang as the initiator of all creation does not satisfy the scientific and philosophical questions before us. The traditional cosmological argument that God is the First Cause no longer works on at least two grounds:

1. The question arises: If God is the First Cause, what caused God? That question is obvious and sophomoric, but the next is more complex.

2. If time and space are not constants, of even distribution throughout, and the same everywhere, how can causation be determined? How can we say that anything causes or is a product of anything else? How can we ultimately attribute responsibility for human actions, fix blame, and assign responsibilities? For instance, if time and space are not the same everywhere, then the determination about the sequence of events—what happened first, second, third, etc.—is impossible except as a description of local phenomena. Ultimate causation thus is impossible, since it depends upon events occurring in sequence, so that the prior event can be said to have produced the next.

The answer, of course, and what preserves a limited doctrine of causation, is that we can make statements about cause under special or limited circumstances. Transcendent and universal statements are not definable; they are usually more useful as rhetoric or polemic. When we make universal statements about cause or infer blame, we can presume that we have lapsed into error. Such statements have more in common with political rhetoric than with morality. We are unable to make meaningful universal statements because we remain contingent beings limited by our human frailty. We are in the image of God, but when we try to speak in universal ways, we aspire to be God. The conclusion is that humility is a useful as well as an admired value. Humility helps to keep us aligned with the reality of our human limitations.

What remains certain, however, is that theology must grapple with the shape of the universe. Theology molds our understanding of cosmology, and our cosmic outlook helps to determine our theology. Theological reflection avoids the doctrine of creation or the prevalent cosmological understanding at the risk of becoming irrelevant. That very doctrine, however, shapes how we think about our neighbor and ourselves. The task of theological reflection is to engage in discourse about the relationship between how we view the universe and how we live together as the people of God.

In addition, interest in the doctrine of creation has increased in recent years because of our concern about the environment. We are slowly recognizing that our theology of creation determines our outlook on the universe and our morality. If we accept that God created the universe, then we become its stewards rather than its rapacious abusers.

Thinking About Human Relationships: A Theology from Below

A "theology from below" begins with humanity and rises toward God. In popular religion, especially in Protestant circles, we hear it in the popular question "What would Jesus do if . . . ?" It begins with loving one's neighbor and understanding that we find Christ in one another. The Old Testament law "Love God and love your neighbor as yourself" is carried over to the Summary of the Law and the work of Christ. Thus Jesus is the man who lives for others, God's sacrifice who embodies the supreme example of human love. We know Christ in our neighbor and through martyrs as well as through the Christian story. Through him we know God.

A "theology from below" is most useful, and it also tends to become humanistic. It begins with the Bible. It centers on our human experience and expands toward the divine. When we are able to seek God in one another, the divine reality takes on a concrete yet transcendental and transforming aspect. It is concrete in the other. It is transcendent because we see God in the multitude of the divine creation. And it transforms because it provides the basis for our own hope and renewal.

A "theology from below" can become too humanistic, however, and thereby either make Jesus so Godlike that we avoid his humanity or so emphasize the heroic in him that we fail to affirm his divinity. There may be the tendency to focus on Jesus as God and forget that God's transcendence is what calls us out of personal and current dilemmas. To focus our faith primarily on Jesus, the God-man, may lead us to forget that God is triune. The symbol of the Trinity is important because the number three takes us out of simplistic dualism. It suggests more than two but does not insist on the numerical limitation of three. The doctrine of the Trinity reminds us that God's energies emerge throughout the creation. We should, therefore, not let our radical monotheism tempt us into a unitary fixation. Theology from below pursued without correction may lead us in that direction.

Theological Reflection and the New Worldview

Our view of the universe, our cosmology, is changing. The same may be said of our ability and need to come to terms with our faith in an age when information is a dominant characteristic. Often simplistic answers to the questions of meaning do not suffice. But academic and philosophical responses to the questions of meaning often fail to respond to the pastoral questions of life's challenges. What we now require are methods that respond to theology in a democratic, sophisticated, caring, yet scientifically appropriate manner. The old circular models are not sufficient, and those that are hierarchical are not acceptable. To return to the previous chapter, what we need is a model that produces the acuity of the diamond but seines like a net, a net that is multidimensional and through which the process of meaning emerges from the ripples of what at first seems but chaos. What I describe may be as ineffable as seining for meaning with a multidimensional net from the ripples of a vast ocean whose limits we cannot fathom. Yet it is as concrete as the way we treat our families, how we love our neighbors, how we treat our enemies, and how we respect the gifts God has bestowed on us.

CHAPTER 3

Theological Reflection— Whose Domain?

From the Cradle to the Grave

Inasmuch as we are conscious beings, we search for the meaning of our existence, and finding that meaning may be defined as the basic quest of theological reflection. Even to the atheist or to those who find meaning in other than traditional religious pursuits, life must have some meaning to be worth living—searching for our god(s). Where we find meaning is where our god(s) reside, so theological reflection is everyone's domain. That brings forth a question that exists for every Christian, however: "Is my faith in God or is it in a false idol?" Imperfect as we are, all of us occasionally pursue idols and, alas, some of us make this mistake most of the time. Those questions repeat themselves in different forms from generation to generation as well as during the various stages of life. From an infant's childlike question "Who is God?" to the complaint of a dying person "Why me?" the questions of life's meaning pursue us like the great proverbial "hound of heaven."

The Judeo-Christian Heritage of Reflection

Theological reflection for Christians is a disciplined inquiry to respond, not to the gods, but to God who is revealed in Christ Jesus, the one, true, and living God who is revealed in the Old Testament. When we seek God who is made known to us in Christ, we seek that which brings love, creativity, reconciliation, and the fulfillment of individual achievement and communal cooperation. We seek atonement, that great unifying factor. We also know that sacrifice and God's redemptive love are what make us whole and allow us to experience the wonders of God's kingdom. All those are fundamental Christian assumptions that are tested daily by life's vicissitudes, temptations, and opportunities.

Theological reflection probably began when the first human beings sought to understand the meaning in their lives. Probably that came first at moments of crisis—the birth of a child, illness, a natural calamity, a time of war, starvation, suffering, or death. But it also developed around the telling of stories that illustrated and created a community of relationship beyond immediate family relationships. We know that a long tradition of stories existed before words were set down on tablets or parchment. We also know that the early people described by the Hebrew Scriptures shared those traditions with their neighbors. Slowly, as writing developed, those traditions were inscribed and enshrined. They became the lore of the people and the tradition of the temple. People were especially trained as scribes to maintain and extend the traditional stories. By producing those writings, they extended the reflective process that others had begun. The stories became the tradition that tells us about ourselves, our neighbors, the universe, God, and about what God expects of us. They eventually became the primary documents of Judeo-Christian theology that the world reveres as the Bible. But that tradition did not cease with the closure of the last biblical book; it continued throughout history and exists today in our own lives. The Bible thus should be considered as an open book rather than as a sealed testament. The story of God's relationship to God's people is not yet concluded. A symbol of that is that disagreement about what documents to include in the Bible remains one of the differences between certain Christian groups.

The Old Testament

The first five books of the Hebrew Testament, known as the Torah, were probably compiled from pre-existent materials. The Jews had been taken to Babylon and were living in exile. Their kingdom had fallen and their lives were changed. Their faith had been linked to the Temple in Jerusalem. Now that was no longer present. To find meaning in this time of perdition, they became a people of the book. As they searched for meaning in their time of suffering and anxiety, they preserved the ancient stories that gave meaning and hope. The compilation of the Torah, therefore, became a very important piece of theological reflection. Although living in an alien culture and surviving under difficult circumstances, the Jews developed the belief that God spoke through the traditions of the people of the land. They looked to the past to interpret their experience and seek God's presence at work. By their reflection on the past, they established the primary questions of theology, questions that continue to provide thoughtful and spiritual insights. The responses evolved into our doctrines of creation, humanity, and God.

The prophetic tradition forms the second major portion of the Hebrew Scriptures. It was not part of the Torah, but prophets also wrote in times of stress. They sought to speak forth what they believed to be the truth. Their messages did not transcend time by foretelling or predicting the future; they pointed out what was, is, and remains true. Their cries for justice echoed through the ages. They sought meaning for their times from within their tradition, and they stretched that tradition to suggest reforms and renewal to a struggling people. By these stories they brought succor to the present and hope for the future. They did not so much prescribe or proscribe for the future as describe a loving relationship with God, a relationship to be forged anew with every generation.

The third major section of the Hebrew Scripture is the Wisdom literature. Wise sayings are not unique to the Christian heritage. They became significant as bearers of the faith and the culture. They also revealed and perpetuated an attitude toward theological reflection. The search for wise statements suggests that one goal of reflection is wisdom—using knowledge to find salvation and meaning by becoming attuned to the morality of the divine will. The Wisdom literature of the Old Testament is a human attempt to tap the creative power of divine wisdom. It seeks a connection with a sapient transcendence that energizes mundane affairs.

The New Testament

The messianic tradition begins in the experience of the Hebrew people. It reaches a climax in the revelation of Jesus Christ described most fully in the Christian or New Testament. Through the existence of God on earth incarnate in the flesh and blood of Christ, and by reaching to God through the sacrificial love of Jesus, theology reached anew for a way to make sense of a universe that frequently does not make sense. Here we find an opportunity to redeem the sins of the guilty. More important, here we encounter an occasion to give meaning to the suffering of the innocent.

The eschatological promise takes us the final step. It begins in the Hebrew tradition and extends to the Christian Testament. Eschatology points to the hope for the future that the messianic message made

possible. Eschatology evokes a Second Coming. The sacrifice of inno-
cence and the expiation of misdeeds point to a future that is more than
a repetition of the past. It is new, for it is the kingdom of God or the
New Jerusalem. Eschatology predicts very little, but it suggests that
while we learn from the past and live in the present, we survive for the
future. God is always before us. Theological reflection thus leads to explore the meaning of creation, sin, penance, repentance, redemption,
faith, and hope. Those themes evoke the great questions of theology
that we will revisit later as part of the process of theological reflection.

What must become our concern, therefore, is the question: Whose
role is it to provide theological reflection, who decides on its validity,
and who should make use of it?

The Role of Church Leaders as Theologians

APOSTLES AND BISHOPS

The apostles were the first interpreters of the Christian faith whose
works have come to us. Those who filled the shoes of the apostles, the
overseers or bishops, soon took on the role of maintaining the purity of
faith on behalf of ecclesiastical institution. It was not, and is not today,
an easy task or process. A combination of legislative activity in councils,
accepted practice, and tradition produced the early authoritative documents of the Church. The Church leaders were those chiefly tasked with
maintaining the truth and providing leadership to the community.[1] As a
result, the early Church quickly developed a hierarchy.

Those responsibilities continue to rest today first in the hands of
the heirs of the apostles, but in a world which is increasingly sophisticated in both knowledge and communication, they are no longer able
to control this practice by fiat, dicta, or legislation by a synod.

The bishops always had a role of maintaining the *consensus fidelium*
(the consent or agreement of the faithful about matters of faith). Today,
in the midst of conflicts, divisions, and suffering, maintaining the *consensus fidelium* is a major task. Since a consensus cannot be imposed im-
periously, it needs to be developed with patience and time. We need a

---

1. Liturgies to ordain a bishop still contain language like "You are called to
guard the faith, unity, and discipline of the Church" as part of the examination of
a candidate.

prepared laity and authentic processes combined with patience and personal contact so that our faith may continue to evolve in its expressions.

The historic tradition in the Churches with centralized leadership—whether the office be called bishop, president, moderator, or area minister—assigns to that office the chief responsibility to maintain the theological well-being of the Church as well as to be the chief pastor. In that role those leaders must be able to reflect as theologians on events as they occur. That becomes especially true during moments of crisis. Perhaps the chief theological role of Church leaders, however, is to provide a healthy venue and practical methods for theological reflection by all people. Rather than promulgating and dictating theological doctrine, their role of authorship might be to open avenues and engender theological growth. In that way their authority might focus upon creating or authoring roles rather than the mere exercise of power through the task of governance.

THE CLERGY

In many traditions the clergy serve as extensions of the office of bishop (the episcopate) or head of a jurisdiction. They may differ in some of their sacramental roles, but the roles of interpreter, teacher, and example, while not restricted to the ordained, are certainly primary to their work. In some traditions, of course, the local church acts as the basic ecclesiastical unit. The oversight functions then accrue to the local pastor, who may be affiliated with other clerics in a loose alliance. In any case, they are the professional ranks of the Church, educated, under discipline, and usually recompensed for their work.

In times of personal or community crisis, the clergy are called to lead the Church's ministry to the congregation. Their responsibilities include helping God's people to understand, come to terms with, and rise beyond the immediate crises. By leading the people in their worship and sacraments, the clergy help meaning emerge in and through the great changes of life from birth to death. God's transcendent presence illuminates, clarifies, and celebrates otherwise absurd particularities. The priestly and pastoral function is important because this is where the responsibility for ritual that expresses the work of the people rests. While the community participates, someone prepared, authorized, and recognized to direct the rites is essential. The liturgical rites, of course, reflect a theological point of view and also impose a reflection on the event to which they refer.

CHAPLAINS

The role of the chaplain is often more personal than that of the parish clergy. Parish clergy have community obligations. Chaplains have an obligation to their sponsor, whether this be a college community, a hospital, a bishop, or an official. Usually the role of the chaplain is less public. Often it is ambiguous and personal, because a chaplain has mixed responsibilities, to both the chaplaincy and the institution. Sometimes these may conflict. As interpreters of theology, chaplains may find it difficult to raise uncomfortable questions. If they do, they may pay a high price, as may church pastors who are frequently perceived as chaplains by their congregations. Examples of this abound.

THE MINISTRY OF DEACONS

Within the Church the title of deacon has had a variety of meanings. In the ancient Church deacons had considerable power as the servants of the community. As we recover the functions of the ministry of the deacon, it becomes obvious that the diaconate or servant ministry makes no sense without theological reflection. The deacons embody ministry through service to others, and it is that kind of servant ministry that ultimately gives all life meaning. Without theology a deacon is a secular attendant, a functionary whose gifts are valued, but whose actions are not seen to have any transcendent significance. Good deeds may result, but there is no examination of the social work in the light of God's redemptive love. That is important because social work—caring for the poor, the sick, the needy, the homeless, the prisoners, and those abandoned by adverse circumstances—is thought to be doing beneficial charitable works, but good works alone do not produce salvation.

A deacon's reflection on the human condition is a servant's reflection, and it is essential that this take place to maintain a dynamic and integrated church community. The renewal of the image and the reality of ministry of the servant or deacon is important in this regard, for it reminds us of the painful and sinful aspects of life. Bringing theological reflection to this helps us to perceive the ubiquity of sin. Like rain, sin befalls the rich and the poor, the educated and the ignorant, the well-intentioned and the ne'er-do-well.

EDUCATORS

In addition to ordained clergy, who usually hold academic degrees, there exist three major groups of persons who qualify as religious educators. The first two—faculties of religion and faculties of theology—are always academicians, although the faculties of theology are also concerned with the faith formation of students. The third major group—religious educators—may be employed on faculties, but they are much more involved in the public application of religious education that takes place in churches, camps, and conferences.

FACULTIES OF RELIGION: ACADEMICIANS

Departments of religion in large universities treat religion as one of the disciplines in the university curriculum. They may include specialists in comparative religion, some specific non-Christian religion, or some aspect of Christianity. In professional matters they tend to be scholars first and believers second. Researchers may be students of religion and yet have no faith whatever or at least not believe in the religion they are studying. Most are more like historians, sociologists, and anthropologists, who view their objects of study from a distance. Nonbelieving students of religion can, of course, produce academic and theoretical dissections of religion; however, by definition they are not able to enter into theological reflection unless they can also enter into the belief system and activity that applies to the theology under scrutiny. To do theological reflection, as distinct from academic research, an inquiring seeker must be open to belief and to activity in support of that belief. In other words, as a Christian I can study Islam, but I am unable to think theologically as a Muslim. This distinction is a key factor of the endeavor of theological reflection. Academic detachment is not theological reflection as described in these pages. Theological reflection is like having to use a language in order to describe it. It does, of course, imply a certain circularity that can make the entire endeavor no more than an ego trip, and that is always the danger.

FACULTIES OF THEOLOGY

Faculties of theology treat various aspects of religion in an academic manner, but ultimately they also belong to the faithful community. While a religion department may exist in a secular or church institution without containing any practicing believers or church members, a faculty of theology constitutes a group of people who practice their faith and hold links to an institutional Church. Nonbelievers have minimal value in a seminary setting.

Faculties of theology have a twofold task. First, there is the disciplined examination of religion through all the historical, philosophical, sociological, linguistic, and anthropological tools. Second, theologians must examine the quality of faith, the emotional as well as the intellectual components, and ultimately the totality of being, the spiritual component. Thus theological schools are concerned with education and formation. Unlike those who pursue religious studies, they are passionately involved with their subject matter. Their course of study is not an impartial question by a disengaged investigator. Theological reflection in this context is vital, and many seminaries have suffered for failing to understand this need. Instead, they have sought to emulate the work of religious studies and thereby have been perceived to have lost their souls.

RELIGIOUS EDUCATORS

Religious or Christian educators are concerned with providing a disciplined religious education, but their primary aim is to help form the people of God to do their ministry. Academic minutiae may seem to be a hindrance to the education and preparation of faithful believers who fill the pews. Yet religious educators must be wary that they do not lead people down the sawdust path of emotional outpouring in lieu of the arid labyrinth of theological formulas.

The religious educator, like the novice master in a monastery, must emphasize spiritual formation and provide the intellectual tools to help that formation to occur. Spiritual formation and Christian education have intellectual as well as emotional components. It means exploring not only the right theology (orthodoxy) but also the right practice of faith (orthopraxis).

THE PEOPLE OF GOD

Thus far I have described various professional roles in the theological enterprise. The base of theology, however, is in the work of the people of God, the people who occupy the territory. Regardless of rank or status, we are all members of the Body of Christ, the people of God, and the theological mirror or reflection rests at the base of our search for meaning. Unless we have totally invested our energies in false idols, such as pleasure, wealth, narcotics, and power, we find meaning in the relationships that bring transcendence and in connections that extend the communion of relationships and love.

CHAPTER 4

Theological Reflection and the People of God

The "people of God" includes everyone—professional theologians and pious believers, nonbelievers and agnostics, Christians and followers of other religious affirmations. We all share certain things in common, among them the need for food and water, shelter, safety, self-fulfillment, and meaning. These needs occur differently at different stages of life. Theological reflection has a different effect on each of these stages.

Life's Phases

We know that human beings develop in phases or stages. Shakespeare called our attention to the development that begins with a "mewling" child[1] who is helpless and concludes with the doddering elderly person who is also helpless. Between birth and death we encounter many stages or phases of life. Physiologists as well as developmental psychologists have described these. James Fowler,[2] a theologian, has adapted the work of Erik Erikson[3] to the study of religion. Erikson suggested a developmental psychology that parallels the physiological stages of human development. More recently others concerned with religious formation have studied the implications of the stages of faith-formation. The special needs we have at various stages affect not only our approach to theology but also how we teach, explore, and embody our theology.

1. William Shakespeare, *As You Like It,* act 2, scene 7, line 137: "All the world's a stage/And all the men and women merely players. . . . At first the infant/Mewling and puking . . ."

2. James W. Fowler, *Becoming Adult, Becoming Christian: Adult Development and Christian Faith,* rev. ed. (San Francisco: Jossey-Bass, 2000).

3. Erik Erikson, *Identity, Youth, and Crisis* (New York: W. W. Norton, 1968).

With different phases of life we have different questions and need different answers both in content and in quality. Our search for meaning begins early with the cries of the child seeking solace. It ends with the gasps of the dying asking for the peace that comes when we join the communion of saints, saying at the moment of death, "Lord, now let your servant depart in peace." Between the beginning and the end is the journey of the pilgrim who progresses through life. It is our journey, and each step has its theological needs and opportunities.

Some Caveats

Several caveats need to be added before looking at individual stages of phases of faith development.

First, they apply to all people, regardless of profession or education.

Second, age is not the only determinative. Some adults may remain at what may be described as an early stage, while some young people may leap rather quickly to later stages. In part, each stage of faith-development is initiated by life's events as well as by a particular age or stage of physiological development.

Third, while there is a kind of progression through each stage to the next, they are not necessarily sequential.

Fourth, no stage is ever completed, and we may, and indeed do, revisit earlier stages of development. Under stress we often regress to earlier phases to find reassurance and comfort. Thus it is not accurate to assume that one level of faith or maturity is superior to another. The child is still in us when we are adults, and elements of the wisdom of age may be observed in a child's unexpected insight.

Finally, it may best be said that the different stages of faith-development describe periods of our lives when certain questions are paramount. This does not mean that other questions do not remain.

Theology and the Child

The earliest phase of life is that of early childhood, and in those especially formative years faith is primarily a function of developing trust and meeting primary needs for food, comfort, and attention. Theological reflection at this earliest phase of life is not formed; nevertheless, little children can sometimes pose some of the most perplexing questions about death, their own creation, or the functions of worship. Fowler, however, suggests that the first stage of faith-development comes at about age four. He has named this the "intuitive stage." The child reacts intuitively to its experiences. Its perception of faith is limited to the interpretation provided by parents and authority figures. Faith is interpreted as a series of episodes judged by whether they are enjoyable or not or whether they invoke a sense of awe. Linkage between episodes and a coherent sense of meaning are generally lacking in the young child. To develop theological thinking at this stage, the best we can offer is to tell the stories of our faith-tradition as stories that are unimpeded by theological interpretations. What we can do is to invoke a sense of participation and awe in ritual and to provide a warm, nurturing environment, which will suggest to the child that the church is a place of wonder, of safety, and of importance. The children will bring their own questions and observations to the stories. If given opportunity, they will evoke their own theology, which on occasion may astonish adults with a profundity not expected of those so young.

Theology and the Early Years of School

Children at this stage of life are often betwixt and between. They may regress, but they can also develop very adult ideas, as they anticipate the next stage of faith-development. In addition, some children at this age may be faced with adult decisions and problems. They still want the safety of the stories of childhood, but they also need opportunities to test, examine, discover, and reflect about what they are learning. They often enjoy tangible ways of portraying the stories of faith, but they can also reflect on what these stories mean and how they affect their lives.

Theology and the Developing Young Adult

Fowler names this phase the "mythic/literal stage." At this stage young people—and this extends to some older adults—perceive faith in heroic and mythic proportions that take on a literal or concrete form. The experience of faith is experiential, very definite, and tends to be interpreted in a literal way. In the background the developing young adult is already struggling with the uncertainty of life-and-death issues. Unless tragic events occur and force an earlier confrontation with the ultimacy of life, the developing young adults interpret the biblical texts and their experience of faith as is. At this stage such Christian formulas as "the body and blood of Christ" may be very difficult to understand, or they may be off-putting. Christmas is much more agreeable than Holy Week and Easter, and theological education may be little more than teaching the basic doctrinal statements so that, knowing the words, they will later be able to understand them. This is a time of participation, but reflection is in the background. It takes place but usually in an informal manner that leaves the participants in control of what they accept and reject without an exterior challenge to their choice.

Theology and the Young Adult

We may enter this phase as teenagers, but we are part of it more fully during the earlier years of adult life. Fowler names this third stage that of "conventional faith." The conventions and expectations of society and significant persons provide a system to interpret and construct reality.

Young adults are more concerned with questions of identity as sexual and creative persons. They do this by evoking hopes and aspirations for the future in the way they decide or fail to decide to prepare for marriage, career, and vocation. They may also do this by clarifying where limitations occur and pushing the boundaries by exploring alternatives, some quite radical and discomforting to those in authority. Questioning those figures and the institutions that sustain them is part of the developmental process.

At this stage rationality is very important, and there exists a preference for sequential linearity, but there is also a sense of discomfort with strictures, especially those in which people did not participate when they were introduced to them. Part of the battle with authority is contradiction between obedience and rebellion.

Theology and the Reproductive Adult

Quite obviously, people can bear children soon after puberty, but this is rightly lamented, since they have not yet asked the questions of life that prepare them to offer a nurturing environment. This stage of life usually occurs after we have identified our vocation and selected a mate. With the responsibility for children there also occurs a desire to join the community in a new way. Among the institutions in our community, church may provide many supports for raising, nurturing, and educating children. Moreover, the children themselves cause people to ask questions in a new way.

At this phase, which Fowler named the "individuative stage," individuals begin to take authority for their own faith in a different way. They also now know that they are responsible for their own actions and may now have responsibility for the well-being of small children and/or elderly parents. This is a time when a systematic and orderly universe may be preferred, and questions of justice and the meaning of evil become predominant. It is a time to choose political parties and to decide what church they will join.

People at the individuative stage of life are joining society and providing nurture for the birth and raising of the next generation. Their questions regarding faith have more to do with selecting where they will find support, assistance, understanding, and activity for themselves and the nurture of their offspring. At this stage people want to know what kind of church they are joining, what they may expect from that church, what it will provide, who the leadership is, whether they will be comfortable with it, and what the cost of membership (discipleship) will demand. They want straight answers and find it difficult to accept ambiguous responses. Individuals at this stage, if pushed on their affirmations, may exhibit great defensiveness. They will declare their affirmations with energy and conviction but possess anxiety concerning a lack of internal certitude. The rise of congregations responding to these needs just when the greatest portion of the United States population reached the age between twenty-five and thirty-five is no accident. It was a response and a product of the needs of a large plurality, the baby-boom generation.

The need for churches to pay attention to this stage, however, is greater than just responding to normal developmental needs. That we live in a mobile society is a cliché. One of the consequences of our mobility is obvious: every time we move to a new environment, we must build new relationships and discover our place in a new community. Some of this is elementary, such as locating a new physician, a lawyer, a banker, and even a favorite grocer. Regardless of age or maturity, the need to establish life anew immediately brings us back to the questions asked at the stage of our early youth. We may even experience some of the same exhilaration about the possibilities, as well as some of the anxieties, concerning the new relationships we need to make. The Church, therefore, needs to be as responsive to veteran church members who relocate as to brand-new converts. They share many of the same needs.

Theology and the Maturing Adult

The maturing adult (average age of around forty-three according to some developmental psychologists) begins when we ask a new set of questions. Having reached approximately half of life, with children needing less nurture and parents approaching the final stages of life, we begin to ask questions revolving around the meaning of life. This is the stage of life that Fowler named the "conjunctive stage," when we begin to allow ambiguities to replace an either/or approach. We begin to be open to our own vulnerabilities and those of others. We become open to the possibility that there may be more than one or two ways to be right, as well as the possibility that life's decisions are not easily made, because there are so many gray areas. This may be a time to reconsider our vocations and our associations. It is a time when many divorces occur, and it may be a time to explore new ways of thinking, acting, and experiencing our religious affirmations.

When we become more committed to a more universal view of the world and reduce our tendencies to oversimplify the views of other people, we enter a time when ministry can acquire a new meaning. At this stage individuals begin to understand that service to others is ministry and that performing ministry gives meaning to life because it provides an outlet for our talents that offers them to and for the world. Sacrifice, giving of ourselves, provides a sense of value, which makes life worthwhile. It is the discovery of our destiny.

A Sophisticated Theology for a Technological Age

Today large numbers of people possess more than a basic education, and many people have made sophisticated preparations for technically complex and intellectually demanding work. We make decisions that are more and more difficult and have greater and greater effect because we have access to powerful tools and techniques. Whether we work in a bank, for a pesticide company, practice medicine, operate specialized equipment, interpret the law, or teach—to name only a few professions— sometimes even without realization, we are faced with life-or-death decisions for ourselves as well as our nearest relatives and associates. And equally important, these decisions also have ramifications for many others whom we will never know. To put it simply, local decisions hold global implications.

Amidst this complexity a child's Sunday school lessons are not sufficient. We live in a sophisticated and complex society that has inherited heterodox cultural heritages, diverse opinions, and a multiplicity of ethnic aspirations. In this maelstrom of crosscurrents, a simplistic faith fails to deliver hope that sustains over the long haul. The opportunity to develop our faith in order to nurture the resources that enable us to live faithfully has become a necessity. That is why it is important to learn about theological reflection and the skills of learning how to think theologically.

In a world that changes rapidly and responds to events like an immense village, and in which all kinds of opportunities as well as disasters loom, many experience a crisis of faith, and almost all of us will encounter those moments of crisis at some occasion. Like death and taxes, moments of crisis are inevitable. The response to these moments may come in at least three ways. Many have lost faith or at least have renounced any ties to organized religion, precisely because the old absolutes failed them. Others have put their faith in a compartment that separates it from the remainder of their lives. These are the well-known Sunday worshipers whose religion does not affect their daily decisions very much. This is the path of avoidance that is not concerned with living a faith that makes creed and action congruent. Still others have made their faith their life's vocation. They presume that any critique that reaches into the basic structures of belief is unfaithful or heretical—something to be avoided, repressed, or even condemned. They are unable to question information they receive from the Church and what they believe without developing intense anxiety; they respond with authoritarian and rigid doctrinal axioms and behavioral requirements. This group often looks with nostalgia to a halcyon past and resists change, while simultaneously vigorously seeking to impose their point of view on others. None of these three groups, however, responds effectively, for they have failed to reflect productively on the meaning of their choices. They have refused to learn to "think theologically."

To develop one's personal theology is one aspect of being faithful to our Lord. To learn to think theologically requires that we avoid dogmatic and idealistic interpretations. It is difficult to engage in an effective reflection when we begin from a position that there is only one "right way," and we know what it is. A person who reflects on his or her personal theology is always a person in the process of change, who knows that God has been there, is present now, but also will appear in new and unexpected ways. The task of knowing God and God's will is always before us. It comes to us both from the record of the past, especially the Scriptures, and also through God's action in the world in the present. We know of God's presence by God's action in the past. We discover God's will by boldly moving into the future. We never know it in advance, but we experience the divine will when we exercise the courage to live with love and courage. Discerning God's presence from the past, living in full sacramental union in the present, and encountering God's will in our hope for the future—these three essences of faith, occurring in a cyclical and continuous flow, represent the essence of theological reflection.

Theology and the Wise Adult

The final or "universalizing stage," according to Fowler, is very rare. It describes a state of being in which the individual has reached a sense of universal understanding of relationship that rises beyond the ecstatic faith-encounter and now exists as a self for others. Some claim that historic figures such as Buddha, Jesus, Gandhi, and Martin Luther King, Jr., manifested this stage. Fowler's interpretation, however, may be too limited. Many people, not just a hero or an international guru, acquire a degree of wisdom. While wisdom may properly be associated with the passage of time and aging, it can also grow out of the young. Perhaps the age of wisdom is better described as that portion of our lives that demonstrates a sense of destiny, self-offering, and openness that allows others to find solace and sapience.

It may be difficult to design an educational methodology for this stage, but I am convinced that there are many people who, in their own way, reach a universalizing stage. These are the wise adults of the community who are no longer engaged in economic battles, the search for power, or begetting the next generation. They possess a lifetime of experience, and they have acquired tools by which to interpret this experience. They now have wisdom to offer, and they have a need to tell their stories. We will do well to again provide a special place in our lives for those who are at the universalizing stage of life. They have much to offer in the way of experience, knowledge, and hope. They have experienced despair and difficulty. They have grown through tragic moments, and they now are most affirmed when they are valued as chroniclers of the past who herald the future.

Who Might Seek to Learn Theological Reflection?

By now the answer to this question should be obvious: *Everyone,* because everyone seeks to find meaning in life. Within the reflective array there are many different areas of specialization as well as different phases of life when particular approaches to thinking theologically are appropriate. While all of us engage in reflection in some way or another, some of us do so more effectively or honestly than others. This book describes some of the tools for reflective thinking. Having the right tools for the task may offer us ways to explore our theological questions and so develop answers in thought, word, and deed.

CHAPTER 5

The Role of Theological Reflection

Once removed from the academy and the dominance of the professional theologian, theological reflection becomes an activity that involves those who fill the pews of our churches. It offers an opportunity to examine some of the most poignant, the deepest, and the most significant aspects of our lives and yet respect the dedication and importance of scholarship.[1] It forms the core of our spirituality, because a spiritual practice is itself a theological reflection that involves all of life.

Theological reflection enters our life at five significant points:

1. engaging the pastoral needs of the people;
2. establishing and maintaining a system that sustains the community of faith;
3. finding meaning and transcendence;
4. energizing the apologetic role;
5. providing correctives.

The Pastoral Role

Historically the Church has recognized four major pastoral functions: healing, sustaining, guiding, and reconciling.[2] Theological reflection touches all of these to some degree, although it provides direct support especially for the functions of sustaining, guiding, and reconciling.

---

1. This is inclusive. It does not exclude the academicians, clerics, and church leaders who are as much a part of the congregation as the laity. It does, however, suggest a certain parity and democracy.

2. William A. Clebsch and Charles R. Jaekle, *Pastoral Care in Historical Perspective* (Northvale, N.J.: Jason Aronson, 1994 [c 1975]).

41

HEALING

The notion of healing presumes that there exists a sense of illness or lack of well-being. Theological reflection as described in these pages deals primarily with the aspects of healing that might be listed as personal care and maintaining well-being rather than healing. Theological reflection is not a therapeutic tool, but it should have a salutary effect. Building communities of support that can develop a sense of meaning and understanding as events, pleasant and unpleasant, unfold is like providing a community with clean water as a means of preventing diseases caused by microbes. Health is improved when theological reflection takes place, because a healthy climate exists. A climate of honesty, support, openness, and charity is the *sine qua non* of theological reflection, and it is the basic sustenance of a caring and supportive community.

SUSTAINING

Theological reflection touches us where we live, at the personal level. It supports us in our needs, at the pastoral level. It makes us aware of the need to provide salve for those in pain, celebration for those who are happy, and protection for those in fear. It makes us aware of the needs of the needy—clothes for the naked, shelter for the homeless, and freedom for those enslaved.

Pastoral theology touches us when we are alone, when we are in the midst of conflict, when we suffer, when we need help with life's burdens. Jesus suffered *for us*. That is the first article of any apologetic for the Church. Thus our first theological task is to make sense of, or at least address, the pastoral aspect of our faith. No matter how philosophically complex or satisfying, any theology that fails to pass a pastoral criterion is invalid.

Theological reflection helps us to cope with what we do not understand. "Why does God allow evil to fall upon the innocent?" That is the ultimate pastoral question, which we often translate personally as "Why me, Lord?" Close behind this question, of course, is "Why do some enjoy unmerited gifts?" The answers to these questions help to form our identity and our sense, or lack of sense, of self-worth.

All these questions are pastoral questions. When we do not have answers, we feel unsupported and lack sustenance. Theological reflection is an important method that pastoral theology can employ to sustain Christians through these great pastoral questions pertaining to the meaning of life.

GUIDING

Pastoral theologians often furnish guidance about specific issues. Advice may be freely given, but that which is truly taken to heart is the advice that is discovered as the answers emerge to someone who poses the questions. The process of theological reflection encourages the development of an internal guidance based on a realistic relationship with neighbors and God. Theological reflection is not the kind of guidance that resolves problems directly, but the insights that may be harvested through effective reflection often lead to productive decisions. Learning to think theologically is akin to learning to fish: it is an art that sustains through time and is more productive than merely providing an answer (a fish) for the problem of the moment.

RECONCILING

Theological reflection may be a way to bring disputes to a fruitful conclusion. That can happen when the parties are able to communicate at least sufficiently to relate their stories without attacking one another and then have the tools by which to examine the underlying meaning. Theological reflection is an excellent means of identifying what differing parties hold in common that can establish a basis for reconciliation. It is also a method that can produce sufficient objectivity so that we can look beyond momentary passions.

One of the important features of theological reflection is that participants need to respect each other's offerings, even when they disagree. Competing beliefs are considered against the backdrop of other conflicts, such as the points of view held by various elements of our cultures and the different perspectives expressed in Holy Scripture. Neither the participants, nor the Bible and religious tradition, nor the cultures in which we participate agree completely on important matters. Placing differences in the forefront of a wide-ranging discussion offers an arena for learning to live with diversities by identifying the common values, pains, aspirations, and commitments we hold. As such, theological reflection can provide a method that develops the reconciling aspects of pastoral theology along new lines.

Maintaining the Communal Contract: Ecclesiology

Theological reflection may eventually lead to the formulation of doctrine. Doctrines begin at the individual level and rise through the various echelons that make up our communities to become historic and global. Doctrines emerge to become expressions that belong to the community, sometimes through adoption by practice and at other times via official ratification.[3] Doctrines are not a set of laws or *dicta* in this context. They are expositions of what may be taught so that the community can maintain its structure, unity, and continuity. Theological reflection is important as a tool to develop the doctrinal contracts that bind our Christian community into a fellowship of faithful believers. Because we share a theology and a language that expresses it, we communicate. We become a community, a church, and we participate in communion.

Making sense of our communal life requires theological reflection at the institutional as well as the personal level. That reflection, in turn, forms, nurtures, and extends the covenant we hold together as members of the Church. Thus our worship or prayer is a primary vehicle for expressing our personal and corporate theology. To be useful, however, those doctrines that belong to the Church must ultimately respond to the pastoral concerns of individual believers. When circumstances change and doctrines no longer sustain or make sense to faithful people, the Church as an institution quickly loses its influence and support.

THE COMMUNITY OF FAITH

The Church is the community of the faithful, and it has some important functions. The Church is the official preserver of the tradition. It bears the primary responsibility to shape the sacramental acts of the faithful. As the administrator of the ecclesiastical structure, the Church possesses the responsibility of accountability, self-examination, and critique to ensure that its work will be well organized and achieved by competent and well-trained persons.

PRESERVING THE CLASSICS OF THE TRADITION[4]

The Bible contains the classical and primary expression of the Christian tradition. Its role has been debated between those Christians who think that all faith comes *only* from the Bible, those who believe it to be without error in every word, and those who recognize that the faithful

---

3. For example, the tradition that the New Testament has twenty-seven books arose by adoption. On the other hand, the so-called Nicene Creed was officially adopted by Church councils.

4. David Tracy introduced this term, and it seems appropriate to use it in this context. David Tracy, *Blessed Rage for Order: The New Pluralism in Theology* (New York: Seabury Press, 1975).

Christian may also look elsewhere for divine inspiration. What no Christian disputes is the primacy of Holy Scripture. The Bible comes first, and the Church has the first (but not the only) responsibility of identifying, preserving, translating, and interpreting its texts. This is an educational task, but it is also a pastoral one that is based on theological reflection.

The classics of Christian tradition, however, incorporate the experience of the people of God beyond the biblical era. The Church has the responsibility of studying and being in contact with this long tradition. Special documents such as creeds and confessions of faith, however, reflect a much larger body of materials that bear the historic tradition and testimony of the Christian experience. They continue the epic saga of how God acts in history to create and redeem the people of God.

Theological reflection is not possible without access to the tradition first expressed in the Bible and then extended as the repository of Christian history. The Church not only maintains these classics, it adds to them. Our experience of God today becomes part of the story that others will treasure tomorrow. The Body of Christ continues through our corporate acts. The Son of God's ministry is our ministry. In the light of new experience the Church continually examines and interprets the past to glean from it God's Word anew. Therefore the Christian classics, far from being static documents, are always made vibrant with new interpretations as well as the development of new materials. The basis for the study of the Christian classics is always a theological reflection that links God's activity with our lives. Our reflections learn from the classics, interpret what we learn, and add to them, so that it may be said that Holy Scripture is a living document that changes and grows with time.

ORDERING THE LITURGICAL LIFE TO SHAPE THE COMMUNITY

Whether the tradition be Catholic and centered on the eucharistic act, or Protestant and centered on the spoken word, or charismatic and centered upon the enthusiastic expressions of worshipers, the worship of the Christian community is where the Church takes shape and maintains its bonds. Worship expresses the tradition and brings the community together, not just as an association of people, but as a communion of saints wedded to God.

The institutional Church has the primary responsibility of providing order to worship. To do this effectively, the officers of the Church must engage in exploring the meaning of every theological affirmation.

They must ensure that the worship life properly reflects, practices, and renews the theology of the Church. They are the primary but not the only keepers of the liturgical tradition. Theological reflection is the development of liturgy, because the conclusions of reflections are the basic building blocks of liturgy. In its simplest form, if the conclusion of a reflection is merely a simple petition to God, we have in hand one of the elements of a traditional collect or prayer. Liturgy is how we celebrate the results of fruitful theological reflection, whether it be over moments of sadness, such as a funeral, or of joy, such as a wedding or baptism.

Meaning and Transcendence

There is much about the search for meaning and the discovery of transcendence in these pages. It recurs here because the ultimate role of theological reflection revolves around that quest. Theological reflection that leads to a dedicated life, which in turn informs our lives and invigorates them with a sense of value, is at the heart of the processes described later. Knowing that life is worthwhile, regardless of our circumstances, is the sustaining element of faith that provides hope, joy, and celebration. These elements are present when we have value for others, when we are ministers. When faith and hope are expressed in our ministry, we experience the transcendent, because we reach beyond our immediate place and time.

APOLOGETICS AND THEOLOGICAL REFLECTION

The traditional task of apologetics is to explain the faith to those who are not believers. Apologetics might be defined as the face of theology that opens to the world at large. Evangelism, then, is the expression of that face as it seeks to convince nonbelievers of the appropriateness of the Christian message. Theological reflection is not an apologetic tool to be used directly toward those who are not part of the Christian family, for theological reflection, as we describe it later in this book, presumes a familiarity and a degree of comfort with some basic Christian affirmations.

Learning to think theologically, however, can make the difference to someone called to express or explain the Christian faith to others who may not be so persuaded. Often liberal Protestants have expressed considerable difficulty in confessing their faith and explaining it to nonbelievers. Others, more strongly persuaded, have been able to proclaim their faith in God and their commitment to Jesus Christ in rather vociferous ways. There is another way: the reflective theology of a congruent life. Theological reflection prepares participants to demonstrate their faith on the basis of their spiritual depth and their charitable activities rather than on arguments and oratory.

Examination and Critique

A wag once suggested, "Show me a theologian and I will show you a heretic." We no longer burn heretics, but heresy still abounds. That is not necessarily because of misdeeds or miscreants. Every heresy emerges from the extension of good theological doctrine beyond its reach and balance. Often, of course, heresy also has a polemical and political aspect.

Heresies have consequences, many of them unfortunate. The institutional Church has a responsibility to ensure that what passes for theology is discussed, examined, and evaluated. This task calls for combining the expertise of the academics with the political acumen of the Church hierarchy and the common sense of the people of God. Disputes over heresies can be crucibles for the development of theology. Such disputes were the raison d'être for many of our primary statements of faith, above all the creeds, which have become an important part of our tradition and our worship life. It is important, therefore, that the Church seek to maintain the dignity of all participants when disputes over theology arise. Even those most mistaken have some proper basis for their conclusions. Even those who turn out to be correct have their faulty points. In theological disputation charity should rule, and this is best achieved through a reflective and consultative process that withholds judgmental declarations in order to find consensus.

Examination and critique are more than the identification and eradication of errors. The Church continually examines its theological affirmations to establish nuances or arrange emendations required by new conditions. For example, the Church once proclaimed a theology that favored slavery. No one would now provide such a theological defense, since our culture recognizes that slavery is indefensibly and fundamentally evil.

The task of theological revision also exists in much less obvious ways. Our language changes and so do our philosophical presuppositions. To make sense, our theological propositions must also be interpreted and stated in new ways for every new generation. Much confusion exists today because traditional theological statements expressed in creeds and confessions are no longer understood. The language and theological presuppositions require translation. The words sound familiar and seem clear, but the framework of philosophical reference is no longer understood; therefore, without interpretation the message is confused. The opportunity to reflect theologically in a responsible and disciplined matter is a requirement if we are to sustain our faith during an era of rapid and unnerving change.

CHAPTER 6

Theological Reflection—
Rationalized or Relational?

Theological Reflection and Social Structures

Social structures like industry and commerce, our educational system, our social agencies, our system of justice, our military command structure, and our churches represent how we think the world works. For instance, when we think mechanistically, we organize our institutions as if they were machines and maintain them by "oiling the cogs" and fueling their engines. On the other hand, if we think organically, we organize as if all the parts are integrated around a core, and we resolve problems by trying to go to the "heart of the matter." Both ways produce certain moral commitments.

In turn, our moral commitments reinforce our social structures, since the predominant presupposition is that destructive or sinful behavior is anything that undermines the validity of our organizational structures. Possessing property, deciding how to allocate work between workers and managers, family relationships, and organizing for major projects depend upon systems that describe and enforce a system on its constituency. Without structures we run into the probability of chaotic self-destruction. If we lack the ability to change our structures, we encounter calcification, which eventually produces a failure to adapt. All this, of course, affects theology and how we proceed with its reflective processes.

"Do our social structures evolve from what we do, or do we act on the basis of the strictures we uphold as vital?" This is a "chicken and egg" quandary. We often presume that our rationale emerged from careful consideration and that we act on that basis, but actually we never know whether our experience determines our structures or whether our structures determine what we do. Cause and effect seem jumbled. Our inheritance, including our genes, our experience, our analysis, our interpretations, and the systems we inhabit, form and inform our lives. They are like the air we breathe, for they pass through us, interact, and affect us even when we do not think about them. Most aspects of our structures or systems and our experience are preset, but we also can claim some freedom if and when our fears and our structures do not control us completely.

Much of our society depends on a rationalized structure gauged to eliminate uncertainty, and our educational patterns often seek to assure the preservation of the status quo. Indeed this is a dilemma for educators. Is education to produce keepers of the tradition? Or is education to produce innovators who think differently and therefore challenge the past and offer new possibilities for the future?

Our reasoned organizational ability has served us well in some aspects and terribly in others. The same system that has eradicated smallpox and has brought us worldwide communications, a bounteous agricultural system, and a multitude of wonderful improvements has also intensified personal strife, war, poverty, and the pollution of air, sea, and land. In summary, we at once glimpse the Promised Land of milk and honey and the hellfire of eternal damnation.

Many use the proclamation of our systemic failures as a focus. They thrive on the energy created by constant anxiety and, on occasion, the outright fear they generate when the media feature "real-life" coverage of calamities and sensational, even lurid, events. Jails filled to overflowing, drug problems, violence in the streets, bombs in our public facilities, threats of disease, and contaminants are but a few of the items in a constant litany. These are omens of a system that is under stress when its limitations are unable to contain what pulses from within. At times it seems that the whole world is embattled.

There is irony in our strife, because the strife that destroys is itself also a sign of hope. We are not totally limited or imprisoned, and there would be no strife if no one cared. Extending the limitations of a system depends upon the deviant, the one who will not play the game according to the rules. The rationalized system under which we live is based on rules or laws that prescribe and proscribe our behavior. The system depends upon a system of crime and punishment to maintain its control and dominance. It is ironic, however, that a rationalized system requires defiant behavior to define itself as well as to provide energy and impetus for adaptation and expansion. In other words, rebellious behavior provides the energy needed to produce new opportunities for learning and growth.

The Potential for Hope

The very stresses we feel suggest the possibilities for something new. Our social structures struggle against the limitations we have imposed on ourselves. Some of those limits are necessary for survival; others smother us or have become inutile. The struggles occur because we are unable to control or even agree on which limits are important for survival and which ones are actually destroying us. Those who wish for change and let the consequences come as they may are the people who feel incarcerated by a system that does not meet their needs. Those who oppose change may see some of the problems, but they fear quite rightly that when one boundary moves, another shifts, and our survival may suddenly be at stake as a sequence of events unfolds like lava engulfing the terrain after a volcanic eruption.

There are other approaches to consider. At the very center of Christianity is the Cross, our symbol of faith that asserts above all that everything is always on the line. Grace is not cheap, and faith cannot be expressed without sacrifice. Christian theology suggests that loving one another rather than ordering with rules is a way to respond to life. In the face of a structure that operates on a basis of desire and dominance or in the face of our human imperfections, a simple proclamation of love is not sufficient.

Theological Reflection: Who Decides?

Thus far we have noted that theological reflection has developed over time and that we may affirm that thinking theologically is a practice that belongs to all people. God is the final arbiter of theology, but in this world that process emerges from the people of God, the communion of saints, the Body of Christ, the Church. That earthly arbiter of theology is not an institution or a set of officials but the assembly of God's people. As we noted earlier, becoming a theologian is a communal task that requires relationships unimpeded by artificial hierarchies intent on maintaining their controlling power.

A productive method for theological reflection is essential to that task of bringing together the reflections of the people of God. To this end, this chapter first describes the rationalized worldview that emerged from our philosophies and that has often blocked the development of a theology by the people of God. The chapter then explores what can happen in seminars to develop a relational approach to the theological challenges we face.

In New Testament terms, the rationalized system that has often dominated Western society is not very different from the law against which Saint Paul railed. The theological response to this system is the way of Christian love. But love is not simply affection and certainly not an emotion. Many emotions accompany the decision to love. There is a way to love: to emphasize relationships rather than rules. Relationships use rules as tools but do not idolize them.

Revelation, Reason, and Relationship

Thomas Aquinas and others distinguished philosophy from theology by suggesting that philosophy begins with natural reason and that theology begins with revelation. But revelation comes through experience. Historical events reveal God's presence to humanity when they are properly understood and interpreted. That interpretation is a theological endeavor which was nearly displaced by science, especially during the nineteenth and the first half of the twentieth century. In the place of religion, a rationalized system has emerged from the combination of a rational philosophy and the natural sciences that dominates the Western world. Although under increasing pressure today, our rationalized systems govern our political, economic, and social structures with an essentially hierarchical and closed system that depends upon a highly rationalized structure for its existence. Before proceeding, it is essential to understand how profoundly the rationalized worldview has both brought great gifts and also hampered human life.

A Rationalized Approach[1]

THE BACKGROUND IN WESTERN THOUGHT

The rationalized worldview can be attributed to three philosophical themes: Idealism, rooted in Plato's worldview;[2] causation, described

1. I am grateful for the seeds and much of the content of this section on rationalized approaches to a presentation made in 1966 by Orin P. South, a management consultant with industry, at the Du Bose Conference, Monteagle, Tennessee. His presentation enabled me to discover how my own education had both prepared me for the rationalized system of the university and also impaired my capacity for creative and innovative thought. I am convinced that today ratio-

by Aristotle;[3] and Nominalism,[4] which developed in the Middle Ages. In this context it is necessary to oversimplify these concepts to make the point. In general, our Western system originates from the combination of these philosophical motifs. To be sure, today that system is under great pressure, and changes that question its limitations are constantly developing.

PLATONIC IDEALISM

Plato believed that what is real is the Ideal. Anything we might see or handle could not be "real" because ultimate reality is defined as what is perfect and eternal. Quite obviously, everything we encounter that is of a terrestrial or human nature changes, rots, rusts, or dissipates, so it could only be an imperfect copy of the Ideal, that which is real. Following Platonism, this meant that the noetic or mental and rational processes

---

nalized theology is ultimately arid and self-destructive because of its rigidity and intent on systemic self-preservation. Rationalized approaches, however, are useful as tools to respond to interim needs to resolve particular problems. The real difficulty with any system is not the system itself but its deification by making it a particular system into an absolute standard. Alas, much of academia remains in this rationalized morass, although it is being challenged by the new possibilities of the information age.

2. Plato (ca. 429–347 B.C.E.) is the philosopher upon whose writings much theology developed, especially during the Church's first millennia.

3. While Aristotle's philosophy had less impact on theology than Plato's, his work was known to the early Church Fathers during the first five centuries of the Common Era. They were rediscovered during the Middle Ages. Aristotle's philosophy is a fundamental factor behind the theology of Thomas Aquinas, who was, of course, also very much under the influence of Plato.

4. Nominalism is associated with several medieval philosopher/theologians. Most noted is William of Ockham (ca. 1290–1349), although the term goes back to the epoch of Peter Abelard (1079–1142). Nominalism pertains to individual entities that can be given a name, hence nominated, from which we derive the term "nominalism." Thus individual and named things were different from universals, which were considered by Nominalists to be mental constructs. This produced a philosophy very distinct from that of Plato and Aristotle and opened the path to modern critical thought. It also produced a wedge between theology, which thought in universal terms, and the critique of a new, emerging philosophy. The philosopher who pursued nominalism was inclined to analysis rather than synthesis. An analytical point of view then opened the way to scientific thinking and laboratory methods based upon experimentation, analysis, and conclusions, to be themselves critiqued in turn. The result was a rationalizing or explaining of phenomena and an ever deeper probing. It led to scientific discoveries and also to biblical criticism, which analyzed the Holy Scriptures.

are the only real and eternal aspects of humanity. To sustain this argument, Plato developed the doctrine of the soul, and he presumed that it survived the human physical presence as the pure human essence.[5]

Plato described this theory in his Allegory of the Cave, a celebrated passage in Book V of *The Republic,* which Plato wrote in the fourth century before the birth of Jesus. Plato also believed that the Ideal was in the mind and that knowledge and thought were the way to reach toward it—hence the high place given to philosophy. Platonic Idealism dominated the Greek intellectual world into which Christianity was born. Since philosophy held a high status, early Christian theologians sought to show how Christianity could compete, and they thus incorporated elements of philosophy into their nascent Christian theology.

Platonic Idealism, modified by Neo-Platonists during the second century of the Christian Era, dominated theological thinking in the early Church and during the Middle Ages, side by side with the development of Church laws or canons by which to enforce the growing body of theological thinking. Church law was based on the legal system of the Roman Empire. Together, Roman Legalism and Platonic Idealism inspired the great theologians of the Middle Ages. They sought to explain the biblical messages about God, Christ, the human condition, and salvation, as well as the significance of their discovery of the philosophy of Aristotle.

CAUSATION

Plato's student Aristotle was as much a student of nature as of philosophy. He analyzed what he observed and categorized it. He also asked why things were as they are. Among other things, he examined the nature of causes and identified four kinds: a formal cause (the plan or purpose by which something happens); a material cause (the contents); a final cause (the purpose); and an efficient cause (that which provides the motive power). The first efficient cause was a First Cause, a term that Thomas Aquinas later identified as a way of describing God. In our Westernized rationalized system, a set of events has to be described as dependent upon the prior event called "the cause." This concept of causation is important to maintain the integrity of a rationalized system,

5. This separation of the soul by Plato has influenced Christian spirituality. Elsewhere I write that the spiritual aspects of our lives, represented by our souls, are not separable from the totality of our existence, which is a notion quite different from that which Platonists would articulate.

since the system depends upon a hierarchy of causes, with the earliest cause to be credited with all that happens subsequently.

NOMINALISM

The third major factor in our Western rationalization is Nominalism, the concept that what is real is what we identify and name (nominate), what we can touch and feel. Ideas are not quite as real as concrete objects, which we can weigh, measure, analyze, and manipulate. This runs counter to Platonic Idealism, which few people today understand because the notion of idealism is foreign to our Western culture.[6] We are Nominalists. The concrete experience is the reality. The ideal is something to which we should strive, but it is always something not yet attained and therefore not the reality of our experience and the world.

How Rationalizations Work

Today there exists a tendency, especially in the West, to think that what is real is what we can feel and that ideas are merely wispy figments in our heads, perhaps even illusions unless supported by an objective and concrete reality. We posit ideals, even utopias, which we then seek to attain, but until they are defined, we understand those ideas to be mere "figments of our imagination." We then presume that we can produce new things by taking one step at a time, each step another achievement that takes us from one concrete reality to the ideal of the next until we complete what we wish to achieve. When working mechanically, such as building a house, this approach is usually fruitful. But if we look closely, we quickly perceive that any creative endeavor takes on its own life, even erecting a well-planned edifice. Our ideal visions are quickly changed, dropped, or even reversed by "commonsense necessities." Our visions did, however, provide the initial seeds. They were the seeds that provided hope for future accomplishments.

Our rationalized worldview is a very busy and productive one. In that respect it resembles a beehive. They are busy places, but beehives have difficulty adapting, and they do not change very much over time. The same was true for many generations of human development when life remained relatively unchanged; but today we find that our communities

6. Platonic Idealism in its purest form is still to be found in Christian Science, whose adherents are the followers of Mary Baker Eddy (1821–1910). Christian Science asserts that healing is promoted through "right thinking," and this is based upon an assumption that the processes of the mind are the ultimate reality.

and their amenities as well as their problems are radically different from the past. For the time being, at least, that trend toward the new and different continues and its pace increases. We are motivated by our ideals, and when one goal is conquered, another confronts us, a factor that can lead to a feeling that life is merely a "rat race." This forces us to center on the task or the mission, even if the path is costly.

This is a rationalization process in full bloom. *Rationalized* people are people driven by goals. They are compulsive. The end justifies the means, because only the end is worthwhile. Of course, sometimes we fail to notice the detritus we leave in our path as we march inexorably to a goal. We focus on the ideal that has been set by a rational plan and fail to account for other unintended, even unseen, consequences. For example, this is what our agony over the spoiling of the land, the sea, and the air is about. We need industry and we need raw materials, so we deface the landscape with mines and denude our forests. Only profits, the benefits of their productivity, motivate us. We fail to see the results that leave a ruined environment—poisoned, deserted, and destroyed—because the ideals of survival and comfort are the desires that dominate.

A Rationalized Schema

A rationalized schema has a logical flow. It emerges from idealism and, step by step, moves to a conclusion that returns to the beginning. It is evolutionary and circular. The logic appears inescapable. The alternative is self-abnegation and submission to the rationalized schema or rebellion leading to revolution. But revolution does not necessarily break the cycle, since there is the tendency to reimpose the rationale into a new cycle. Thus the politics of the extreme left and extreme right, with their strong ideals, are products of the same rationalized system. As the French cynic who commented after the rise of rationalism said, "The more it changes, the more it stays the same."

A rationalized system contains certain characteristics. The first is its notion of the ideal person who is:

Rational
Logical
Practical
Controls all emotions
Balanced
Knowledgeable

An Ideal Person will:

> Ask intelligent questions
> Explore familiar patterns
> Rely on experience to make decisions
> Depend on "provable" assertions
> Be intellectually involved
> Search for commonsense solutions
> Prefer the middle of the road position
> Try to relate the whole to its constituent parts
> Prefer an authoritative establishment
> Insist on a strong chain of command
> Rely on competition to motivate

An Ideal Person will not:

> Admit ignorance easily
> Search for intuitive patterns
> Rely on feelings
> Prefer new theories
> Select an extreme position
> Work with unanalyzed wholes

From this listing it is possible to extrapolate what it means to be an Ideal Theologian who uses a rationalized approach. The Ideal Theologian:

> Studies and understands classical philosophy and theology
> Offers a logical and acceptable set of doctrines
> Worships in a calm and predictable pattern
> Knows and seeks to follow the doctrines of the Church that are rooted in the past
> Selects authoritative sources for faith
> Applies faith to everyday life

An Ideal Theologian working in a rationalized system will:

> Insist on clear statements of dogma and doctrine
> Rely on prior expressions of faith
> Analyze imagery rather than contemplate it
> Seek proof-texts from Scripture and other authoritative writings, such as canon law and confessions of faith
> Demand obedience to the ecclesiastical authorities
> Venerate the old and the traditional

Understand spiritual as a faithful characteristic that removes the individual from a sordid life; one rises from the sins of the flesh in order to discover the gifts of the spirit

Perceive sin to be the violation of the law

Search for universal solutions that apply to everyone

Specialize in specific areas of interest

Be careful to identify different branches of Christianity

Perceive Christian groups to be competitive

The Ideal Theologian will not:

Find it easy to understand the meaning of grace

Perceive law and dogma as descriptions (they are prescriptions and proscriptions)

Consider spirituality as dealing with the whole person

Understand the community as the source of authority

Admit quickly that the Church and its leaders can err unless in conflict, in which case the opponents, of course, are those in error

THE CONSEQUENCES OF A RATIONALIZED APPROACH

When either Ideal Persons or Theologians go to work, certain things result. First they live in constant interpersonal tension. They are part of a society in conflict that worships the past and focuses on the future. They find it difficult to exist in the present; a sense of guilt is often present and, coupled with anger, can be seen in the gloom and depression, which must be constantly pushed aside. Conflict is a nearly constant state that both depresses and energizes.

The results of an idealized and rationalized system are a dynamic and active society that exists in tension, emphasizes sameness, and insists on competition. It rewards those who "obey" the rules but idolizes those who refuse the rules successfully and test the system. When they prove the system "wrong," they return from the fray to the renewed system as heroes.[7] The alternatives are either to rationalize and deny the pain of existence or to revolt, and then install a new system. For the reli-

---

7. The role of violence in our society and its relationship to sacrifice play an interesting part in this cycle of institutional repression, rebellion followed by a new institution that changes everything and yet does not alter its pattern. This is explored by René Girard, *Violence and the Sacred*, trans. Patrick Gregory (Baltimore: John Hopkins University Press, 1979). An interesting follow-up is to be found in Gil Bailie, *Violence Unveiled* (New York: Crossroad, 1995).

gious life the choices are stark: either one must insist that all the old expressions of faith are correct, or one must revolt by establishing new sects, denominations, or religions. The rise of a multitude of Protestant denominations is a textbook for those seeking to maintain a rationalized system that is unable to contain the fervor and energy of its citizens or control the power of God. New monastic communities seem to serve the same function in the Roman Catholic Church

THE BENEFITS OF A RATIONALIZED APPROACH

Since a rationalized approach is goal-oriented, it is also productive. Military conquests and landing on the moon are products of rationalized systems that have been very successful. So is the conquest of polio and the World Wide Web. A rationalized system urges a focus on the promise of the future as a means of coping with the deprivation and pain of the present; however, if one looks closely, the great strides that made success possible were often intuitive rather than derived from logical reasoning.

Religious groups that insist on a strong eschatological expression are rationalized even if they are fundamentalists. Indeed, fundamentalism and literalism are highly rationalized approaches that require considerable intellectual expertise to uphold. We err when we attribute literalism only to the uneducated or the emotionally deprived. Cleaving to a strong authority represented by a literal approach is an expression of rationality, although it may appear unreasonable or at least illogical.

Fear, however, is the fundamental factor in a rationalized system. Fear drives people to hold on to the system at all costs. Rationalizations are ways to avoid change, to affirm what they already know, to delude themselves into believing that they can control what will happen, and to provide order when they fear that chaos is imminent and that it is inevitably destructive. Since the fundamental motivation behind a rationalizing system is fear, attacks on the system only compound the fear. Fear is the essence of resistance to a system that serves some aspects of life quite well, namely, maintaining the status quo, because the system offers an illusion of immortality. The fundamental factor, therefore, is fear driven by a desire to avoid an ultimate (yet inevitable) ending, the conclusion or death of what once had life.

THE PRICE OF A RATIONALIZED SYSTEM

What are the costs of a rationalized system? One word suffices—pain. Our society demonstrates how much pain we suffer not only by the advertisements for analgesics but also by our abuse of drugs, alcohol, and our insatiable need for diversion and fantasy. A rationalized society is a society in pain because it is always in tension and in competition. Somehow, if we do not use painkillers or distraction, we withstand the pain with the cultural norm of a stiff upper lip or the false promise of immortality.

A rationalized society needs enemies or it must develop them from inside. There must always be another mountain to conquer, a fight to win, an opponent to better. Our sports are our most civilized opportunity to cope with this, but when we view the remains of shattered gladiators on the football field, we should remember that even there the price is high.

A rationalized society has winners and losers. It is important that we can see those who fail so that those who win can enjoy their triumph. Leaving people without shelter on the streets fills a certain need. When we see the failures, we who do not lack have an opportunity to feel good and also have a reminder to work hard. Society's castoffs are a problem only for those who approach them with compassion or find them an irritant. For those who support the system, they are reminders of the penalty that accrues to those who do not join the club and play according to the rules.

THE ABUSES OF A RATIONALIZED SYSTEM

The costs of a rationalized system point to what many see as abuses. This price is not a new factor, for the world has known abusive systems from the left and the right. During the last century two great rationalized systems, Marxism and fascism, provided paradigmatic examples. Abuses occur whenever those who hold the reins of power become so enthralled by their denial of reality and so fearfully bonded to their need to maintain the system at all costs that any perceived enemy is systematically eradicated. Whether the enemy is the little recalcitrant farmer in the Ukraine or the Jew in the ghetto, or whether it is someone of another race, national origin, sexual orientation, or language, in a system based on fear, that enemy must be conquered and eradicated. Every rationalized system, no matter how humane at the outset and how well balanced by checks and balances against its own tyranny, can become abusive under the pressure of fear.

What is important to learn is that the system is flawed, because its basis is in fear. Basically good people, acting out of fear and ritualizing their response into a systematic social structure, tend to produce a system that is abusive. The common denominator is not race or language or sex or educational level, but fear. Fear leads to a desire for domination. Fear leads to cataclysmic revolutions. Fear undermines the potential for creativity. Unfortunately, our educational systems have often used the very same rationalized approach and have depended on fear as a motivator. Students compete for grades and scholarly recognition. The fear of failure is an ever-present dynamic, with the consequent devaluation of the loser. Success is lauded and rewarded.

THE NEED FOR COUNTERVAILING FORCES

When we live in a rationalized system, the driving force may be fear, but the immediate impetus arises through a desire to achieve, to win, to conquer, and to become "number one." A rationalized worldview needs a continuing flow of obstacles. The conquest is always of the others, and this is achieved by a perception that the world is made of dualities, me and the other, one person pitted against another (others), like a fighter in the ring.

THE BOON AND THE BANE OF DUALISM

Dualities help us to discern. They provide depth. That is why we perceive better if we have two eyes and two ears. Dynamic dualism works on the basis of a dialectic, one always in motion toward a goal or purpose—finding the ultimate single ideal. We always seek to bring things together, but to have something to bring together, we first assure ourselves of a plentiful supply of contraries eligible to be brought together. Dualities also help us to differentiate. I learn who I am when I discover my distinct characteristics and when I note how I differ from others.

Dualities are useful tools, but in theology, certainly in Christian theological education, dualities are dangerous tools, for they easily lead to simplistic conclusions that easily become tyrannical ideals. Ideals imposed as absolutes become tools for domination. Perhaps that is why absolutes are best left to the divine milieu. All the ideals we are able to know are evoked through human beings, so they are at least a little bit flawed and therefore do not qualify as absolutes.

Among theologians who employ dialectics—arguing one point against its contrary to arrive at a synthesis—there is the risk of arriving at ideals that become the basis for a system that will enslave, corrupt, and destroy. Dialectics are useful tools, but they become dangerous when they become the only way to solve problems. They are useful educational tools, but they should not be determinative for the way we approach the decisions of our lives. As such, the dialectical approach is not the appropriate manner to pursue a theological reflection.

IDEALISM AND PROPAGANDA

When an idealistic government rules, whether in politics or in other structures, and the dynamics of a rationalized system dominate, the tensions mount rapidly. Stress becomes a major factor, and one way to combat that stress is to deny reality. Governments do this by both placating the public and using propaganda. Propaganda seeks to delude so that the game of avoidance can be played. Rationalized approaches rooted in idealism usually are the first to sacrifice honesty in the name of truth. Those who deviate, question, or work to alter the system become traitors, and the degree of punishment meted out is directly proportionate to the degree of unreality that exists in the system. Trust becomes the great and unfortunate casualty.

THE CHURCH AND RATIONALIZED SYSTEMS

The Church often falls into the pitfalls of establishing rationalized systems. Theologians and clerics in turn have developed theological positions to sustain such approaches. The work of developing a theology has often been assigned to talented individuals who became respected because of their position in the structure. Discipline has often been used to attempt to keep everyone in line within the systems developed by the philosopher/theologians. Of course, none of this has worked very well, which is why we have a proliferation of denominations, sects, and religious groups. Where once the Church condemned heretics to the hands of the state for execution or exile, now we depart from one another and organize new coteries of like-minded people, who then develop their system, their tensions, and their divisions. It makes for a depressing outlook, unless there is a recognition that amidst all this there are also some other ways to approach the problems.

A Relational Approach

THE ORIGIN OF A RELATIONAL APPROACH

A relational approach depends upon the interaction of the participants in a community. The community is at the base of all relationships.

Its origin is as old as humanity and the need to live together for the common survival, benefit, and happiness of any society. We do not live alone very well, even if solitude is something we occasionally crave.

As Christians, we recognize the importance of the community. We know that communion—coming together to share with one another—is at the heart of our religious practice. We may come into this world alone and depart from it alone, but we live together, and that coming and going affect and involve others. Where others are, so is God, so the commandment to love God and neighbor is not simply a rule but a statement about the necessities of our existence.

THE CHARACTERISTICS OF A RELATIONAL APPROACH

The ideals of a rationalized system are expressed in proscriptive or prescriptive terms that take on the nature of being absolute qualifications. In contrast, a relational approach cannot be diagrammed neatly into a flow chart, nor is its shape anything close to an absolute. A relational approach maintains flexibility. To keep a structure in place means that participants must communicate, check out what works, make changes, be open to critiques, and refrain from judging new ideas too quickly. Members of a community in relationship live in a network in which their place is determined by functions and skills rather than by appointment, money, or power.

To maintain the community, members work with reality, always checking with one another and building on what precedes. In a rationalized system, often the job must be mated to the structure, but in a relational approach the structures change to suit the goals of the community and the job at hand. Major changes or challenges are met by increasing or improving skills. Working relationships and networks determine authority. Roles are not fixed, and tasks are engaged cooperatively. The main problem is the difficulty and the time needed to maintain the flow of communications essential to the relationships. The emphasis is on meaning rather than on precision according to closely articulated definitions. The meaning includes the emotional, spiritual, physical, and intellectual aspects of life.

THE BENEFITS OF A RELATIONAL APPROACH

Authenticity is a major benefit of a relational approach. To maintain the community truth, candid communications must be available. This is a contradiction to the rationalized system, which thrives on maintaining a competitive ethic and so values protective secrecy in order to maintain a winning edge. Winning against others is not the goal of a relationship. Winning for one means all win, because the conquest is against those things that prevent life, liberty, and the pursuit of happiness rather than the defeat of others.

When we seek to live in relationship, individual identity is a personal as well as a community problem. When relationships are important, the community is at its best when individuals are most creative and able to develop their personal potential for their own as well as the common good. Individuals are integrated into the community without demanding that everything be homogenized or made alike. The organization exists for the benefits of its members, and the purpose is the well-being of everyone in the community.

THE COST OF RELATIONALITY

Relational approaches require time and patience. They do not always respond well in crisis because the entire community needs to be brought on board. As a result, a community that is organized in a relational manner must undertake a great deal of preventative planning so that it can be quickly galvanized to deal with crises. Since there is no unitary leadership to act decisively under pressure, the initiative can be lost and the community can be destroyed because it could not respond in the face of disaster.

THE ABUSES OF RELATIONALITY

Communities working on the basis of relationships are innovative and creative, but they can also be abused. The individual who has no conscience is not only unwelcome in any community, but if relationships are the basis of the community, that individual can destroy it. A relational community is open to the abuse of those without conscience, and if that tendency becomes dominant, such a community can become highly destructive and undisciplined. A regard for the well-being of others is essential in any community. Unfortunately, a community rooted in love has a difficult time expelling or disciplining its deviant and destructive members.

RELATIONAL APPROACHES AND THEOLOGICAL REFLECTION

From a relational approach a theology emerges that looks somewhat different from much that has been done in the past. Gone is the authoritarian theology derived from academics and the Church hierarchy as the sole arbiters of the meaning of faith. Doctrines are not laws to be imposed but descriptions of beliefs to be taught. As faith grows and changes, so must its doctrinal descriptions.

If theology is relational, then it must exist within a community of belief. Our goal is to work out our relationships so that we build community. We know that often our actions (sin) disrupt our community. Confession becomes our means of opening the lines of communication, and forgiveness means at least that we provide the opportunity to renew our bonds. The spiritual life becomes more than a solitary meditation. It is the expression of our self-awareness as we work out our relationship with ourselves, with our neighbors, and with God. While we recognize the importance of individual salvation, we know that it happens within the context of our community, which will not allow for simplistic answers that eliminate opportunities for large groups.

Finally, in a relational approach theological education seeks to increase skills for the present rather than prepare scholars according to past models. Here rests the tension between what schools do and what the world wants from those who graduate. What the Church structure and the academic world must remember is that new challenges are to be met with new training, new ministries, and new adaptations.

What I have described as a relational approach is in fact a description of much that is happening. One of the products of the inevitable confrontation is conflict. Within the Church there are those who seek to be flexible and then encounter those who are fearful, who would prefer to cleave to what has been tried and found useful in the past.

Theology has always sat on the edge of two precipices—one of maintaining the tradition and the other of living with the demands of the present as it gives way to the future. If it gives in to tradition, theology becomes a relic for the museum. If it gives into the latest fad or demand, theology can no longer articulate its gifts with an authentic voice. When we engage in theological reflection, we seek to maintain the balance so that our faith does not fall into a worship of the past nor abandon its roots and seek to live only in the present, as if nothing else matters and no hope outside the "now" exists. In our communal relationship, Christian theological reflection is a product of the people of God. The work of the specialists is important, but the task of finding the meaning of God in our lives belongs to all God's people. Thus it is appropriate that our preparation to live in a complex world that demands much of us should include a preparation in theology. Just as we must learn something about how to keep our bodies well and how to express our talents with creative activity, we must also have an opportunity to develop our faith. Just as a grade school education cannot prepare us for professional employment, the Sunday school education of a child cannot sustain us as adults.

PART II

Theological Reflection
The Educational Context

CHAPTER 7

Theological Reflection
Education in Depth

The Need for Community

A reflection incorporated in a disciplined fashion as part of an educational program can carry a student well beyond the process of imparting information. It provokes profound questions. The answers that may be derived and the decisions that ensue have the potential of touching all areas of life. That is especially true when that reflective process takes on a theological character that has the potential to involve the human character at its deepest and most personal levels.

The importance of reflection in our lives cannot be underrated, but it may be misunderstood. In popular parlance we sometimes say that we want to "take time to reflect." That usually means time to be alone, perhaps even close our eyes and ears to external stimuli, and ponder information or events as we "think it through," so that the reflection remains a personal and internal process. This is like looking in an illusionary mirror by imagining what we will see but never actually using a reflective surface. Internal and personal reflections are important and valid, but they are not quite properly reflections, since the very notion of reflection suggests an independent feedback, as a reflective surface provides feedback.

Theological reflection requires a community that acts as a reflecting medium. A community can provide responses through a process of reflection if the climate for reflection is secure and supportive. In fact, all our human interactions with others (when two or three are together, there is a community) provide feedback, some verbal, some through tonalities, some through appearance and posture, some conscious and intended, and some subconscious and subliminal. What we pick through these reflective stimuli causes us to adjust, consciously and unconsciously, what we say and do.

A community participates in the developments of its members through the reflective loop that grows as we share ourselves with one another and learn. It works best when the messages are clear and the loop is an open one, always ready to integrate something new. It serves us poorly when communications are garbled and the loop is closed, so that we repeatedly look only at the same data without learning anything new. Of course, such a process of reflection, some of it productive and some of it destructive, goes on in any community or group, often in an almost automatic way. Much of the time it is beneficial or neutral, but it can be painful and even destructive. Gossip, of course, is an example of the latter, while honoring good deeds is an example of the former. Because much of the feedback we receive is not disciplined and there is no opportunity to examine it in a supportive environment, unfortunate conclusions sometimes result, or else what might be truly helpful is filtered out by the personal defenses of the ego. In other words, nothing is learned.

The unpleasant aspects of reflection occur in part because any reflection is always a partial truth. Even looking in a mirror is not totally accurate because the mirror itself reverses the image and also contains anomalies that distort the images we perceive. When we gain the benefits of others' reflection, the message is inevitably skewed by the words that are used, by the viewpoint represented, and sometimes through purposeful malice. The best corrective is a continued dialogue of checking and rechecking until consensus is reached.

To provide some rationality to the reflective processes, we can identify certain aspects of reflection.

Reflection as an Intellectual Proposition

The intellectual pursuits of education are usually assumed to be reflective by nature. The laboratory method of experimentation and observation that may lead to conclusions is in itself a reflective process. Theological reflection can be informed by such practices, because it too is an intellectual pursuit. This means that theological reflection must be as careful as any scientific endeavor to define its terms with precision, to observe phenomena with care, and to withhold conclusions that are not well founded. Theology, like the natural sciences, has sometimes cleaved to old assumptions and conclusions. The result is that it plays the role of a fool in the face of indisputable new information. Two classic cases for theological foolishness, of course, are the discussions about the nature of the universe and the origin of human life. The first came to the fore-front when Galileo was condemned in the seventeenth century for ar-guing that the earth moves around the sun with other planets that also possessed moons. The second is more recent and came to public atten-tion in a celebrated trial about evolution.[1]

Reflection as an Emotional Experience

One often hears the phrase, "I feel that . . ." What comes after "that" is usually a conclusion or opinion, in the form of a thought, judg-ment, or idea, but the trigger for the memory is the recollection of an emotion. Emotions are complex and powerful. The way we speak about them may be direct as in "I am mad," or "I am glad" (the other most basic emotions are sadness and fear). Or we nuance emotions with phrases such as, "I feel distressed," or "I feel uneasy." The power of emotions is that they often provide conscious as well as subconscious drivers for de-cisions. They are also pegs that we employ to recall information. The contents or data of a strong emotional experience will be remembered vividly. When we express emotions we become more vulnerable, so often we express rationalizations that provide some distance between the emo-tion that serves as a trigger and what we assert. The rationalizations serve as a protective sheath.

Emotions are very important to the learning process. Events about which we have no emotional attachment are difficult if not impossible to recollect. There also exists the factor that powerful yet unpleasant experiences may be completely "forgotten" or repressed. Unfortunately repressed emotions can erupt when we least expect them. Flashbacks thus are omens of past souvenirs that were not truly erased from our emotional memories. Reflection, especially theological reflection that touches on some of the more fundamental aspects of life, is a trigger for emotions as well as information that were repressed and thus unavail-able to our consciousness.

---

1. In 1925 John T. Scopes was accused of teaching that human beings evolved from earlier species, thereby violating Tennessee law that stated that it was unlaw-ful to deny that human beings were produced through divine creation. The cele-brated trial in Dayton, Tennessee, ran for eleven days. While Scopes was convicted, the religious conservatives were put on the defensive by the highly public "mon-key trial." The Tennessee law, however, remained on the books until 1967.

In any case, when reflecting on our lives so that our theology can develop, it is important to include the emotional component. Reflection, therefore, is much more than an intellectual or analytical exercise. It can have a very healing or beneficial effect. Reflection in theological education is not, however, a therapy and should not be considered for this. Therapy implies diagnosis, a course of treatment, and a desired outcome. None of these judgments, which should be made only by an authorized person such as a physician, is appropriate as part of theological reflection. Although a therapeutic setting may use theological reflection as part of its work, it is not appropriate for those engaged in developing theology to extend their work into the therapeutic aspects, which are best left to other professionals.

Reflection as an Autonomic Process

Our autonomic processes are those that occur without thought—actions like breathing, the beating of our heart, and the blinking of our eyes to keep them moistened. But reflections also occur automatically, and they happen all the time. As we continually process information about what occurs around us, our autonomic processes filter that information. For instance, we may filter background noise so that we can heed a conversation. Somehow our processes of observation note the noise and "turn it off." This phenomenon allows people who live in noisy areas, such as near an airport, to say that they no longer "hear" or wake up when a low-flying plane passes overhead.

While autonomic reflections are extremely useful, they may also be a stumbling block. What we filter may be of value. One of the products of reflecting in a community is that we can help one another see what would otherwise be lost due to our own filters.

Reflection as a Form of Spirituality

Spirituality involves our thoughts, our feelings, and our activities. Reflection on our lives that encompasses these three dimensions of human existence is a form of spirituality. By being honest with ourselves about what we do, feel, and think, we prepare ourselves to be in the divine presence.

When theological reflection becomes an integrative reflection of intellect, emotion, and action, we are truly engaging our spirituality. This is that level of life at which we set our deepest aspirations and are called to our most important activities. Engagement in theological reflection may produce profound changes that have lifelong implications and most truly demonstrate our values, hopes, loves, and commitments.

Theological reflection, however, should not be confused with spiritual direction. A spiritual director may guide a client with theological reflections, but the work of a spiritual director is itself a specialized endeavor that requires more than what may be learned by engaging in theological reflection.

The Search for Meaning: Seeking Transcendence

STORYTELLING

Telling stories among adults has become popular again, and today numerous storytelling festivals exist. This has ancient roots for communities that were oriented around the hearth. Telling stories has long been an avenue for entertainment, passing on the lore, and most important, maintaining a sense of community. Thus telling our stories is a basic endeavor for any educational enterprise. It is the first step on the path to profound learning and change.

Probably the art of telling a story effectively attained its zenith in the form of the great epic poems of antiquity. Today we tell our stories in many ways. From mythic reenactments in small villages to gossip on the telephone, to the soap operas on television, to the electronic media and E-mail that connect across the globe, telling our stories remains important. When we tell our stories we reach out to others, we make ourselves vulnerable, and we also take the first step toward transcending our local limitations. As we tell our stories, that action itself begins the process of reflection and is an important aspect of theological reflection.

Somehow, telling our story, from the simple cry of a hungry child to writing a complex autobiography, is the first step to moving away from being alone. We tell our stories differently to different people, because we take into account the experience and the reactions of others and because we change. By sharing our story we begin to transcend, or at least move away from, the event we describe. Storytelling is the first step in reflection because telling our story means that we must think about what happens, find terms to express it to specific listeners, and discover that we tell our stories differently to different people. Telling the story is different from the event itself. If we look further, we will find that people who share the same event together will relate different reports in similar but quite different ways. Each report will be unique.

Moreover, the same person will not provide exactly the same report twice in a row. Finally, telling and hearing stories are experiences themselves. They are separated from but connected to the events that form the story's contents. The very activity of sharing stories relates us to others, so that we can begin to make the transcendent connections as we seek access to the transcendent milieu.

Telling a story and hearing a story are always ephemeral experiences. The word, like the air passing over the sand, is wispy, but it leaves a residue. You can tell the grains have been blown and rearranged by the effect of the wind. The words we express relate us to the past, project us to the future, and give meaning to the present. Beyond telling a story, however, we must also make sense of that story. We must seek its meaning by studying the relationship of its components as well as how it relates to our faith, our culture, and our lives.

The other component of storytelling is the art of listening. Instructors ask students to pay attention and listen, but they do not teach how to listen. Stories reveal a great deal. A focus on the words and contents is to heed only a part of the message, for our stories contain texts beyond the immediate words. Often, as we narrate an event, our tonality, posture, word choices, constructions, emphases, and pauses reveal a great deal. Some of that message is subconscious and unintended, but it is also part of the story. As we listen we need to be open to the contents as well as the subtexts. Even this, however, is not sufficient. We bring our own history and our own inevitable prejudgments, even if we truly do not intend to be prejudiced. Effective listening requires those hearing an account to withhold judgment. They must seek clarification and check out their conclusions rather than utter denials, confrontations, accusations, or conclusive responses.

MYTHOLOGY

A myth is not a false story, although the term is sometimes used with that as its intended meaning. Nor is a myth true like a newspaper account. It is a megastory. Myths are essential tools of theology because mythology is that which forms a bridge from the realm of human existence to the kingdom of God. They deliver messages about our identity, our destiny, and our relationship to the divine, to the creation, and to one another. Our mythology is how we know who we are and what God expects from us. When the great mythic stories are shared from one generation to the next, they form the foundation stories for our community. Being a theologian requires us to think clearly and to reason. It also requires us to be artists, because the artist is the person who develops the symbols/metaphors/stories that express our relationships, which become the bridges or communications that bind us together.

A great taboo exists among Christian educators, namely, their fear to discuss the importance and meaning of myth. Perhaps this is because we fear the reaction of faithful believers who seek a less complicated presentation of their faith. Too many think that considering the biblical message as a Christian myth is to evoke a denial of the Christian message, something akin to atheism and blasphemy. Even when we know differently, we still have fears that others will perceive our study of Christian mythology as a denial of faith. In actuality, it is the exalted expression of our beliefs. Christian theologians in antiquity, including the prophets and the apostles, interpreted Scriptures allegorically. They used myths to express the reality of the transcendent Christ. Historical events, when they take on a transcendent order, become part of our mythology. In the words of Philip Wheelwright, myths are "a complex of stories . . . which for various reasons, human beings regard as demonstrators of the inner meaning of the universe and of human life."[2] Joseph Campbell offers an even more compelling understanding of mythology:

> The first function of a mythology is to reconcile waking consciousness to the *mysterium tremendum et fascinans* of this universe as it is. The second [function of mythology] being to render an interpretative total image of the same, as known to the contemporary consciousness. Shakespeare's definition of the function of his art, "to hold as 'twere, the mirror up to nature," is thus equally a definition of mythology. It is the revelation to waking consciousness of the powers of its own sustaining source. A third function, however, is the enforcement of a moral order: the shaping of the individual to the requirements of his geographically and historically conditioned social group, and here an actual break from nature may ensue. . . . The rise and fall of civilizations in the long, broad course of history can be seen to have been largely a function of the integrity and cogency of their supporting canons of myth; for not authority but inspiration is the motivator, a builder and transformer of civilization. A mythological canon is an

2. Philip Wheelwright, *Metaphor and Reality*, 2nd ed. (Bloomington, Ind.: Midland Books, 1968) 239.

organization of symbols, ineffable in import, by which the energies of aspiration are evoked and gathered toward a focus. The fourth and most vital, most critical function of a mythology, then, is to foster the centering and unfolding of the individual in integrity, in accord with d) himself (the microcosm), c) his culture (the mesocosm), b) the Universe (the macrocosm), and a) that awesome ultimate mastery which is both beyond and within himself and all things.[3]

Mythology expresses some important functions for us and it is appropriate in that context to think of Christian mythology as a necessary element of our theology. Christian mythology points us to the transcendent truth by awakening us through worship and study to a sense of awe, gratitude, and even rapture in our relationship to God and the fact that God created us. Christian myths allow us to understand the world around us in accordance with our faith and the best knowledge available. Our Christian myths support our Christian order and provide us with a medium by which we can teach future generations the wonders of God's gifts of creation and salvation.[4] Through myth our theological reflections plumb depths not otherwise attainable.

The Christian tradition combines history and myth so that it is at once both immanent and transcendent. The genius of Christianity is the

---

3. Joseph Campbell, *The Masks of God: Creative Mythology* (New York: Penguin Books, rept. 1978) 4–6. See also Gerald Clarke, "The Need for New Myths," *Time* (January 17, 1972). Clarke reviews Campbell's contribution and states:

> To begin with, through its rites and imagery it (myth) wakens and maintains in the individual a sense of awe, gratitude and even rapture, rather than fear, in relation to the mystery of the universe and of man's own existence within it.
>
> Secondly, a mythology offers man a comprehensive understandable image of the world around him, roughly in accord with the best scientific knowledge of the time. In symbolic form, it tells him what his universe looks like and where he belongs in it.
>
> The third function of a living mythology is to support the social order through rites and rituals that will impress and mold the young.
>
> The fourth and . . . most important function of mythology is to guide the individual, stage by stage, through the inevitable psychological crises of a useful life: from the childhood condition of dependency through the traumas of adolescence and the trials of adulthood to, finally, the deathbed.

See also Campbell, *The Power of Myth* (New York: Doubleday, 1988) 31.

4. Joseph Campbell evokes this pattern, which applies to Christian as well as non-Christian myths, especially if it is assumed that everyone has a mythology, even those who claim no faith. See Campbell, *The Masks of God*, 4–6.

Incarnation that includes God and humanity, completely linked, and abiding to redeem evil and suffering. The Christian story is at once human and divine, natural and supernatural, historical, and eternal. It is a hard-fought equilibrium, but this balance makes Christian theology unique. Ultimately it is an educational mechanism, one that extends to the length, breadth, and depth of our existence.

CHAPTER 8

Theological Reflection and Educational Methods

A Critique of Educational Methodology

How should we pass on knowledge from one generation to the next? How can we develop what we already know and produce knowledge that was not available to prior generations? The first pertains to learning and the second to discovery. But the two are intertwined. Often rote learning is a chore and discovery is exciting. Yet much of our educational process turns the joy of discovery into a chore, so that bright-eyed students arrive at school and are quickly discouraged by a system that fails to encourage the joyous experience of education as a process of discovery. The chore of going to school becomes something to dread, and the expectation of a vacation is a sign of hope. Emotional patterns arise to block learning; often these persist as the child becomes an adult. The experience for too many has been devalued almost from the beginning because of our collective memories, which hold unpleasant recollections of hours of ennui while waiting for the next recess or athletic event.

Mortimer Adler, known for chairing the board of editors of the *Encyclopaedia Britannica,* has criticized American education for depending too much on imparting information and failing to teach the meaning of what is taught. He has also worked extensively to help educators look anew at how we teach. As chairman of the Paideia Group,[1] he pointed to the conclusion that we need to look again at how we teach our young. This had implications for the education of adults and

---

1. Mortimer J. Adler, *The Paideia Proposal: An Educational Manifesto* (New York: Macmillan, 1982) 29.

especially for teaching theology. This elite group of educators criticized traditional educational methods that relied on presentations (usually lectures) and educational values that emphasized the imparting of information because they failed to develop a sense of the meaning and importance of that information.

When educational methods help us to make learning a journey of discovery, the process arouses the interests and energizes the students. Often this is best achieved in a seminar or discussion group. In such a venue it is easier to stimulate the imagination so that creative and inquisitive powers may be awakened.[2] Theological reflection as presented in these pages is a format to organize a conversation and stimulate a process of discovery. It uses the format of a seminar and provides the structure to guide that conversation. That structure serves best as a venue in which to discover the meaning, significance, and value of the knowledge that is acquired.

Educators have frequently disregarded the benefits of the interaction possible in seminars, an undervalued and misunderstood modality for education. They have valued the inculcation of data over the joy of discovery, thereby filling minds with information but leaving the individual knowledgeable yet uneducated. They have failed to provide an opportunity to understand or apply data, and they have robbed students of the creative urge to learn. Thus our schools have left many students bored and unmotivated. While the spark may be rekindled later for some, many have remained in an educational lethargy for the remainder of their lives. Adler concludes that we can do better.

The Three Basic Methods of Education

The Paideia Group suggests that there are three basic methods of education: lecture/presentation, coaching, and seminar.[3] The lecture method provides means to communicate the acquisition of organized information. Coaching encourages the opportunity to develop skills, intellectual and physical. The seminar, however, is a forum where the understanding of values and ideas is enlarged and where the process of learning is that of discovery.

The Paideia Group, however, failed to identify a fourth mode of learning—that of meditation, the path to self-discovery. Time to reflect

2. Ibid.
3. Mortimer Adler, *The Paideia Program* (New York: Macmillan, 1984) 8.

usually suggests a religious connotation or at least a spiritual dimension. Its lack reflects the lack of acceptance and credibility of the spiritual dimension in our public discourses.[4]

The Presentation or Lecture Form

A lecture or presentation is what most people accept as the primary educational process. An expert relates either orally or by other media what the student should learn. The student pores over, learns, and comes to terms with the materials. Finally, the student demonstrates mastery over the "contents" of the discipline. Competitive examinations and grades become measures of and incentives for progress. Such a process has certain advantages, but it also has significant shortcomings. The dominance of the lecture-hall approach comes out of a rationalized and mechanized system discussed in an earlier chapter. Thus it is at once dynamic, self-fulfilling, and tension-producing. As a result, many academic courses lack immediacy, purpose, and application. The student's primary motivation can become grades rather than learning the disciplines, and there often exists the mistaken assumption that grades are a true measure of learning. Since winning the game of grades is important, cheating is a consequent and recurring problem. The system frequently operates either on the basis of guilt, fear, and punishment or on a system of rewards and promises. Honesty and study for the pleasure of discovery and the improvement of life should provide sufficient fulfillment, but such ideals do not offer enough satisfaction in an educational world dominated by power and competition.

In a lecture the student is the prisoner of the interest and viewpoint of the instructor. The student may recoil and reject what is offered, but usually passivity rules. "Be quiet and take good notes" is a standard admonition. Students who talk back and argue are usually not appreciated by faculties, who have their own program, agenda, and schedule. God forbid that a student should actually find a teacher making a mistake.[5]

4. For example, we would not expect a physics professor or a historian to suggest that the class should take fifteen minutes of quiet time to ponder and think about the contents of the lecture.

5. Students who "act up" are not appreciated by teachers. While individual problems may be at the root, educators are usually not willing to examine the possibility that systemic problems are producing problems at the weakest point. The most troubled student will probably "act out" first when the systemic pressures become too great. Examples of systemic pressures may be competition, unrealistic

Faculty members who encourage exchanges, on the other hand, frequently complain that the students are not responsive. They have been well programmed to "play the game" that leads to success and rewards.

Lectures are oriented to the future. They open the way to possibilities but do not immediately engage the student in activity, although this is sometimes remedied with homework or laboratory assignments.

While a presenter may invoke humor, offer dialogue with the audience, or promote opportunities for questions, general interchange between listeners in a lecture hall disrupts the process of the lecture. Such tactics are useful to retain attention, but they cannot continue lest the basic educational method is lost.

Information is provided by the teacher that will help with the next examination, prepare the student for the next course, the next job, or events later in life. Lectures that introduce students to a subject for future use are both important and valid, but when immediacy is lacking, the emotional motivation to concentrate and recall the subject matter may also be absent.

The educational task is not complete until there also develops a change in behavior and an understanding of the ideas and values appropriated from the presentations. The promise of future use offers poor motivation for learning, as are fear of failure at examinations, poor grades, and recrimination from parental or other authority figures. Ultimately the best motivators are enthusiasm and participation. These come with involvement, something often difficult to achieve in a student who has become the passive recipient of someone else's lecture.

The Role of Presentations/Lectures

Critiquing our dependency on presentational methods of education should not convey the conclusion that they should not be used. Presentations work best to provide information and to prepare or set the stage for other activities. Presentation or lectures are essential, as are all other types of educational methods, but they are not sufficient or complete. Our educational system may have erred by relying so greatly on the lecture/presentation method and giving it the highest priority and accolade. Perhaps lecture hours should be no more and no less important than practice time, laboratories, seminars, or opportunities to meditate.

---

demands, and expectations to perform in ways that are problematic, such as reading requirements for people who may have difficulties doing so.

Presentations have an important educational function, and for that reason presentations or lectures should be prepared with care. Illustrations should be encouraged, and the materials ought to be carefully organized. Ultimately, good lectures are works of art. They must be theatrical in their appeal as well as academically sound. They must entertain as well as instruct. They must spark the imagination. That is why the best lecturers know that they must balance drama and comedy while conveying their material.

Organization, enthusiasm for a topic, knowledge of the subject, and an effective delivery are essential to make a presentation lively. We would do well in education to teach the oratorical skills that can galvanize an audience. Proper coaching, which provides an opportunity to practice and receive a critique for future presenters, should be encouraged. This process should be a continuous part of our discipline. Lecturers need feedback on a routine basis so that they are encouraged rather than threatened. Every lecturer can benefit from a coach or observer who can signal from the sidelines when the lecture is flat and who can assist in the debriefing later. Contrary to most present practices that encourage lectures to be solo performances, we should consider making presentations and lectures a team effort.

Coaching

Coaching is a second method of education. That is what takes place on the athletic field, in writing assignments, or in laboratories. A task is put before the student, and under the guidance of a competent coach, the student practices the steps and acquires the skills that lead to mastery of certain activities. Coaching always requires activity, which is why sports can be so popular, especially for those who do not succeed at the game of academic presentations and examinations.

Teaching skills only by lectures is not sufficient. The student needs more than information to develop a new skill. The trainee must practice the activity to become adept, and a competent coach is essential. With coaching come demonstrations, the opportunity to test one's skills, and an occasion for critique and practice. One's belief system and theoretical thinking are secondary when being coached, although they may interfere. For instance, someone who suffers a fear of high places may find this a block to learning how to parachute. The activity is what counts, however, and feelings must be faced, overcome, or momentarily ignored to learn through coaching.

Coaching is on-the-job training or learning by doing. It is an essential component of learning. After all, who would want to fly with a pilot who had read his instructions from a book and never flown an airplane under supervision? How well could anyone learn to play a sport or a musical instrument by reading a manual on the subject without ever having an opportunity to practice on the instrument itself? Coaching and practice teach the muscles and nerves as well as the mind, and they incorporate the entire person into the learning process, especially the emotions that are aroused by activities.

On the other hand, being technically adroit can be nothing more than what any robot can perform. In athletics, as in art, there is a need for self-expression, and this comes only when the presentation has meaning for both the artist and the audience. The opportunity to form one's belief system as a result of engaging in an activity is always there. Those beliefs provide a setting by which to interpret the meaning of our actions. Physical activity involves us totally, so it is natural to form beliefs appropriate to sustain that activity. That is why former athletes think in metaphors appropriate to their moments of glory, and former generals think in terms of the arts of war when they bring their administrative skills to civilian activities or the corporate boardroom.[6]

What we do and what happens to us help to form the belief systems that dictate what we are willing to do. While intellectual adventures may inform us, our basic beliefs are usually set in the concrete expressions of human experience. That is why we may become so rigid. If seeing is believing, doing formalizes those beliefs. We have become invested in our beliefs because we have acted on their bases.

Paradigms of beliefs that develop in the midst of intense activity can be very difficult to abandon, for they become precious tokens of special moments. Unless there is an opportunity to develop relationships and a sense of meaning and purpose to a new situation, we will tend to reuse old paradigms even when our experience tells us that they are not working.[7]

6. A good example occurred during the war against Iraq when the American commanding officer, General Norman Schwartzkopf, described his military tactics as a "Hail Mary pass." This expression comes from football, in which he had participated during his college days.

7. Holding on to what we believe we learned under moments of high emotions is the basis for irrational fears that may sometimes govern our lives. When the event that produced the fear occurred at an early age or when it is too painful, it may

Coaching is best used to teach someone "how to do something." It is skill-training, practice with feedback, and support. It offers constant evaluation and reenforcement. A coach works best when the student-coach relationship is strong. Depending on the nature of the task, that relationship may be warm and friendly or even fearful and hostile. To be effective, whatever the emotional tie, it must be strong. Usually fear and hostility can develop the relationship quickly, but with real limitations. A warm, trusting atmosphere can build long and fruitful relationships, although this takes longer, because trust must be built first. But the method depends upon the task, the urgency, and the willingness to accept all the outcomes. Great coaching relationships sometimes begin in fear, anger, and hostility. As the fruits of the relationship are enjoyed, they may develop into lifelong friendships as the value of what is learned is perceived, and trust develops on a new basis of respect because coach and student experience the fruition of their commitments. The driving factor, however, is the emotional bond.

Seminars

One best transcends individual moments by developing a metaphorical discourse. This enterprise may be done in dialogue or in solitude. Monastic retreats are for those who find this best done alone, but even a solitary meditation depends upon reminiscences that involve our engagement with the world and the people we know. Seminars or discussion groups are the most suitable settings in which to seek that transcendence in community. It is here that life's events can be reported safely, illuminated, enhanced, and even made holy by bringing them into conjunction with the other stories of the people of God.

The methodology of the seminar, according to Adler's Paideia Program, is that of the Socratic method, raising questions that are open-ended and provoke thought. The preset agenda of the lecture and the task orientation of the laboratory may lack the ability to convey the sense of discovery and exploration possible in the seminar setting. In the seminar a student interacts with peers to challenge and be challenged, to offer insights and discover the wisdom of others, and to have an opportunity for self-expression and growth. In this arena one discov-

---

remain repressed and guide our behavior even though we are unaware of the origin of the belief that dominates it. Working to find meaning in seminars may occasionally uncover such passed moments, and thus it may produce both great fears and very freeing results. This is not the purpose of a seminar, but it may be a result nevertheless.

ers meaning, because what is learned is set in relationship to the student's life and to what others have experienced.

Often seminars suffer a poor reputation in educational circles because they are thought to be dull or second-rate experiences. That academia sees them of lesser value than lectures is evident. A three-hour-credit course means three hours of lecture, but a three-hour seminar usually nets only one hour of credit on the transcript.

The seminar's low reputation is rational, even if mistaken. Left to its usual devices, seminar sessions occasionally succeed and become very significant opportunities for learning and growth. All too often, however, they degrade into one of several unsatisfactory modalities. In some cases a seminar becomes a lecture (research paper) presented by a student. Usually the quality is inferior to what a competent professor might offer, and there may ensue a lackadaisical and polite discussion. In other words, the seminar becomes an unsatisfactory variant of the classroom lecture with discussion or a practicum for neophyte lecturers.

On some occasions seminars become verbal brawls. Some faculties encourage such sparring in the belief that disputation facilitates learning. Two or three participants launch into heated exchanges that are exhilarating for the participants but rather dull for the onlookers. They are not so deeply moved by the subject, do not wish to be emotionally involved, or see through the "devil's advocate" position that launched the argument in the first place. An effective seminar is not just a discussion group, nor is it a place for debates. Both techniques promise limited productivity.

In general, teaching faculties do not know how to structure seminars so that they can become useful learning situations, nor do they understand the dynamics of functional and dysfunctional groups. At the university level, in particular, future educators are not taught about educational methods, nor do they learn about the dynamics that are found in any group or community. When the seminar is a happy and creative experience, everyone rejoices and marvels at the miracle, but probably the participants and the leaders are unaware of the underlying dynamics that made the experience so fruitful. When the experience is painful, the participants pray for a quick end and hope that they will not be subject to other similar experiences. They often fail to understand the failure in terms of its dynamics. Usually it is not permissible to examine the process and the quality of the interactions, and the experiences are not perceived as part of a normal process that may be studied, controlled, and improved. Instead, often someone is made the scapegoat or problem that made life difficult for everyone. Knowing and having confidence in the elements of the process is the most helpful tool one can possess in order to survive unpleasant experiences. The knowledge of the process can give meaning to what is otherwise strange and perhaps even bizarre, such as the explosion of anger or the withdrawal of some participants into an impenetrable silence.

Elements of the Seminar Method

Contrary to popular thought, a seminar does not just happen. Effective methods to structure and guide a seminar are as important as good technique is for coaching or oratorical skills for a good lecture. A seminar must be created, and its activity must be nurtured so that it can become a safe and useful place to learn and explore. That is particularly true when delving into the theological disciplines, but it can apply to almost any learning situation.

Thoughtful educators/theologians know that theology is a communal affair and that in community there resides the possibility for the creative teaching of theological subjects. Theology, after all, deals with the "stuff of life" (our relationship to God, the universe, one another, and ourselves). In a microcosm of the small group there naturally exists an arena for learning from experience. Learning in the context of a seminar becomes successful by applying a disciplined methodology under the leadership of a competent group leader.[8]

A seminar requires more than a group of people asking open-ended (Socratic) questions and pondering thoughtful answers in a maieutic (maternally supportive) environment. In this regard, the authors of the Paideia Program are naïve. A plan to assure a systematic flow and flexible movement makes it possible to offer data for study, examine the information, draw useful conclusions, elicit implications, and make decisions

---

8. One frequent mistake in structuring seminars is having only one group leader. If the content is highly emotional or personal as well as intense, there should be two leaders for each group of eight to twelve persons. This allows one person to be involved and perhaps caught up in the process and one to observe, protect the participants, and guide the process so that it will be productive. Groups should be kept relatively small so that there is sufficient "air time" (time to talk) allowed to each participant, but they should be large enough so that the group contains different points of view, learning styles, and personality traits to produce natural congruence and dissonance.

for the future. Such a plan must ensure that the processes always at work in a group are given their place and that the leadership recognizes the nuances and meaning of the group's interactions. The methods of theological reflection presented in later pages are ways to structure a seminar. They are also ways to encourage the mentor/instructor to be a facilitator among peers on a pilgrimage of discovery rather than a sage or a guru on a throne.

What the Student Brings and Needs

THE STUDENT'S GIFTS

The very basis of education is that every human being has a natural potential for learning. Motivation of the desire to learn is the ingredient that is so often absent. What we know is that significant learning does take place when a student perceives that the subject matter is relevant to her or his purpose. Teaching to a student's interest rather than professorial or institutional needs usually brings much better results. This means that the students must be allowed to participate in their education, not as recipients only, but as partners in the learning/teaching process.

Real learning takes place when one can and does act differently as a result of what has been learned. Learning involves a change in self-organization as well as self-perception. That kind of change also incurs new responsibilities. It is threatening, and so resistance to learning is normal. In theological terms, when we learn something new, our ignorant self dies and a new, now informed self arises. Needless to say, as a result of this repeated death-and-resurrection experience as we encounter the teaching/learning process, we find that education is assimilated more easily when external threats are minimized. One goal of a seminar is to maintain a safe environment to facilitate the learning process.

We know that we learn more easily when the whole person is engaged emotionally as well as intellectually with action. Theology, at first glance, is an intellectual process, but it emerges from our deeds. To make the learning lasting and pervasive, the methodology needs to help students discover the theology of their deeds. This kind of self-critical approach has an evaluative undertone. To learn from our actions, evaluation by others must be of secondary importance to maintaining the safety of the learning venue.[9]

9. Carl R. Rogers, *Freedom to Learn* (Columbus, Ohio: Charles E. Merrill, 1969) 152ff.

LEARNING STYLES

The Appendix at the end of this book presents a series of methods for theological reflection. All the methods emerge from the same set of theories and use the same model to organize the sources. But the methods for reflection have different purposes. Therefore they begin at different points, move along different paths, and appeal to different users. Selecting a method may well depend upon the needs of the participants in the reflection and how they learn best. Not everyone learns best in the same fashion. One aspect of a student's security in the educational situation is determined by a congruence between the educator's teaching style and the student's learning style. A variety of methods need to be used in a seminar, because different people have different ways or styles for learning.

Some people are better able to visualize the information, others learn better through the aural pathways, and still others need to be kinetically involved. Somehow a seminar's pattern of reflection needs to be attractive to all three so that we can hear, see, and experience (perhaps only vicariously) the learning experience.

In addition, there are generally four basic learning styles, according to Anthony Gregorc's Mind Styles Method.[10] The first two learning styles prefer highly personal experiences but eventually move reluctantly to theorizing or seeing the larger picture. They are:

- Concrete Sequential: A preference for learning definite and concretely physically experienced information offered in an orderly and organized presentation. Prefers literal meaning and likes labels. Uses language in a succinct and logical manner.
- Concrete Random: A preference for learning definite and concretely physically experienced information, organized by the recipient, often in three-dimensional patterns. Uses lively and colorful language so that words do not always convey the real meaning of the message.

Two other learning styles prefer the world of ideas expressed in abstract or theoretical terms but eventually seek definite experience once the theory is described. These are:

---

10. There are a number of ways to ascertain learning styles. One of the most popular ways is found in Anthony F. Gregorc, *Gregorc Style Delineator: A Self-Assessment Instrument for Adults* (Columbia, Conn.: Gregorc Associates, Inc., 1985).

- Abstract Sequential: A preference for abstract ideas or theory based upon a concrete existence offered in an orderly and organized presentation. Highly verbal and uses polysyllabic words and enjoys precise rational language.
- Abstract Random: A preference for learning theory that is then organized by the recipient, often in weblike multidimensional patterns. Uses metaphoric language, gestures, body language and colorful arrays.

The significance of learning styles for seminar participants and leaders is great. First each leader or mentor needs to recognize his or her own style, for this will affect the way he or she exercises leadership. Most people can work effectively in more than one style, and almost everyone has one style they find particularly problematic. When learning complex information, it is difficult to do so in a style that is most clearly the one disliked. If we need the subject to be presented concretely and it is presented in an abstract manner, or vice versa, we just do not get the message. Having knowledge of these educational conundrums can be especially helpful when communications continually break down. Looking at a disparity between learning and teaching styles may explain the problem, so that personality conflicts are avoided and constructive correctives may be offered. While it is difficult to teach or to learn in a style not your own, it is possible to make adjustments or seek assistance. Knowledge of the problem is the first step to a corrective.

CHAPTER 9

Theological Reflection
An Educational Adventure

Adventure, the discovery of the unknown or at least the opportunity for new experiences, is part of what makes life interesting and exciting. We discover new things as we encounter them, examine them, and bring them into relationships that illuminate and energize our lives. The work of theological reflection is an exploration. At its best it contains all the energy, anxiety, and hope that accompany the discovery of new worlds. Opening ourselves to a process of reflection is also an adventure. It entails certain risks as well as opportunities. What we discover may confirm what we already know, it may give a new perspective, or it may even overturn well-established presumptions and set us on a new course.

Levels of Discourse

While discoveries may touch us most deeply at the personal level, they also affect other aspects of our lives, such as our homes, our professions, and our friendships. Each aspect of our lives has its own discourse, because it has its own subject matter, its own values, and its own vernacular. Although the various discourses use the same language—in this case English—as their primary vehicle, the patterns of thought among them can vary greatly. It might be quite possible for the expressions of one discourse to be incomprehensible to someone who does not belong to the group that uses a particular discourse. In other words, every discipline has its technical language, and that language is jargon to those outside the discourse of that discipline. Some refer to these as levels of discourse and consider the most technical to be the highest or at least the most complex and erudite. Within the context of theological reflection, that judgment may be mistaken.

The Fundamental Level of Discourse

The most fundamental discourse is personal and exclusive, the discourse of our private thoughts and prayers, but it is like a battery that needs recharging from time to time. It requires an external connection where the energy for the discourse and its language originate—our interaction with the world and our interactions with others in our Christian community. While theology often emanates from the work of scholars or preachers, the primary level of theology is in the work of the people, and the most basic element is the individual with a theology rooted in a personal faith. Everyone has some means of making sense of the world and what it means. With each attempt to derive answers, knowingly or naively, we build our personal theology. It first emerges out of two sources—the discourse that takes place in the faithful community and the personal and private discourse that follows our interactions.

In addition, secondary discourses may be identified. Chief among them is our discourse with the wider world, the public discourses that involve institutions and their sustenance. A more specialized discourse is the engagement with a particular discipline that emerges from a technical and professional stance. So, for example, my personal beliefs and my interaction with others about them reflect a discourse at a primary level. Sermons, creeds, liturgies are discourse that belongs in the public arena. A presentation about systematic theology or biblical studies falls in the province of professional and technical discourses.

One of the pitfalls of theological reflection, or any reflection for that matter, is that we confuse discourses and trust that all is said in the same manner, with equal value and with the same meaning. A preacher who uses the technical language of theology on Sunday morning will probably be ineffective. That is obvious. But confusing our own understanding (belief) with what is preached in public or what is taught in academia also produces difficulties. For instance, some years ago, when theologians publicly uttered the phrase "God is dead," they were speaking out of a technical and academic discourse that failed to communicate to the people who filled the pews on Sunday. The results were a flood of words and arguments, an avalanche of books and articles, and a general lack of comprehension, marked by vituperation, headlines, and defensive publications.[1]

1. The controversy over the phrase "The death of God" occurred during the 1960s. The idea was not new, but the publicity it received remains a landmark of

Clarity about the discourse and the community that uses theological cal reflection may make it more useful as well as less frustrating. It is complex, however, since the same words, used in different contexts, frequently convey different nuances and, sometimes, very different meanings. A little word like "sin" can serve as a good example. At the personal level my sin is what I think I have done wrong, feel guilt about, should confess, and seek forgiveness for. At the institutional level, sin is what produces the inevitable destruction of a life that knows no love. But sin can also be described as "missing one's mark" or failing to attain a goal. Still another definition for sin is the engagement in the ugly and evil for personal gratification, for which we usually reserve the term "porno," as in pornography. Finally, sin may be defined theologically as disobedience to the divine will. This does not exhaust the possibilities for how to interpret the meaning of "sin," but it does illustrate the potential for confusion and misunderstanding.

Our Personal Theology: The First Level of Discourse

THE PERSONAL QUEST: INTROSPECTION

At its most personal, theology is an internal dialogue, a search for God within, a discourse between the individual and the divine. Wise counselors can help with spiritual advice, but ultimately this part of our lives is between God and the self. It can be a very lonely course. It can also be a very dark course, as some of the mystics have testified. In a sense, this is the quest for the mystical, something we sometimes avoid lest it take us places we would not wish to visit. What we harvest from the quest for the mystical shapes our interaction with the world, sometimes consciously, sometimes unconsciously, for our internal dialogues are like tapes that play in the background of our consciousness. Their messages may only emerge after lengthy meditations, through guidance or in our dreams. Sometimes they erupt as a revelation, a true and surprising moment of insight.

Meditation, personal prayer, and contemplation are the building blocks for our personal theological discourse. By using them we en-

---

the failure to bridge popular religion and academic nuances. People perceived it as an attack on the divine. Theologians intended it as a statement of reality that expressed the state of the world that had become secular and scientific. See Thomas W. Ogletree, *The Death of God Controversy* (Nashville: Abingdon Press, 1966).

counter life at its most basic, and we encounter God in a most personal manner. We derive meaning from what is otherwise confusing and troubling. We also find it in the graceful moments when we encounter the numinous, perhaps when awake, but also in reveries or dreams. Meaning may be imposed from the exterior, but ultimately it requires an interior validation that comes with personal meditation. In turn, from the interior of our souls new gleanings can emerge that may be shared and can take on mystical proportions that have the power of revelation when and if they are affirmed by the world.

The mystical has always been a source of theological insights. Quite different from a scientific or academic quest, the mystical seeks to reach beyond what we already know for a glimpse of the reflection of God's light on what we do not yet know. That may be information, but usually it is more about understanding, making sense, seeing old things through new glasses, discovering new paradigms.

THE FAITHFUL COMMUNITY: THE PRIMARY LEVEL OF DISCOURSE

As described in this book, theological reflection is primarily a process that takes place within the community of faithful believers. While it affects the personal, internal, and mystical, it really is about the development of a culture that thinks theologically. Theological reflection within the community of faith is about developing tools for the interactions that make this possible. Its discourse centers around the cycles of life and how these interact with different aspects of community life. This kind of discourse is localized, because its references will be to local persons, events, places, and memories that may not be known outside of the immediate community. It will have its own jokes, fears, songs, expressions, slang, and mores. Nevertheless, even if it is not Christian in its perception, it involves personal interactions that revolve around two aspects of life, the predictable and the surprise. Predictable aspects are cyclical, like birthdays, anniversaries, and paying taxes; the surprise elements are the moments of crisis, those events that are not part of the normal flow. Accidents, earthquakes, or even pleasant experiences, such as winning the lottery, fall under the genre of surprises.

Primary-level discourses are conversations that lead to results. They are formative for the participants, who discover the meaning of their lives by means of the intellectual and emotional exchange. Theological reflection needs to begin at this level first so that it can truly be a worthwhile endeavor.

The Larger Community: The Public Discourse

THE DISCOURSE OF THE MARKETPLACE

Public discourses are communal and, therefore, of common concern. They belong to the marketplace. The most common public discourse is that centered on the issues of governance—economics and politics. Political discourse covers a host of topics. These include marketing, financing, public relations, provisions for education and culture, protecting the community, and organizing the community for the common good. Politics, however, are never far removed from the discourse of commerce and finances. Ethnic, ethical, and aesthetic concerns are the other kinds of public discourses. These concerns usually rise and fall in importance and may mask other interests, such as a desire for power or economic gains.

SERMONS, CHURCH PRONOUNCEMENTS, CONVENTIONS, CREEDS

The public discourses of theology are usually in the form of sermons, religious pronouncements, confessions of faith, creeds, and doctrinal statements. When a community engages in theological reflection, it may be productive to examine the public discourse of a particular religion. A comparison of the public discourse of that religion with personal practice of individuals, or the public discourse of the larger community or other religions, is useful. Here too, however, what we do with our resources, usually determined by finances, offers the best information about the values our communities maintain.

The Discourses of Academia

RESEARCH AND SCHOLARSHIP

The professional or academic community usually presumes that theological reflection reaches its highest level when scholars research, study, analyze, and interpret the documents of our faith on behalf of the community of faith. Certainly great scholars of the past, as well as more recent thinkers, have reflected deeply about the meaning of theology within the confines of academic scholarship. Scientific research into all aspects of theology has been and remains essential and valuable.

The prevailing presumption is that academic theologians, touched by their own experience, are the most important interpreters of theology for the Church. They must be free to experiment, to test, to make mistakes. That presumption, however, may be ready for evaluation and a new careful interpretation. While it is not possible, for instance, for the average person to learn Greek, Latin, Aramaic, Hebrew, and Syriac and become an expert in early Church history, it is possible to become knowledgeable about theology. The increased education and sophistication of educated professionals who are lay theologians are not to be taken lightly. More and more the average person is forced to become conversant with the disciplines of accounting, law, and medicine to manage his or her personal life. To fail in this is to be left to the mercy of unscrupulous professionals in these areas. On that basis there is no reason why the public should not become sophisticated, if not as theologians, then at least to acquire a comfort level with their faith amid a turbulent world.

The questions and the opportunities before us, therefore, revolve around the following: (1) How do adults in a complex society achieve the theological sophistication that is commensurate with the general level of education they have received? (2) How can the theology we provide to educated laity be offered so that it forms a helpful corrective and support to the difficult decisions that must be made? This is especially critical in a very complex world where a few people can wield great power and in which all of us have the fearful opportunity of creating great damage with something as mundane and readily available as our automobiles.

Methods of Theological Reflection

We engage in theological reflection in a number of ways. Our first engagement is with what we do (praxis). Our second reflective engagement is demonstrated by what we worship (liturgy). And our third engagement with theological reflection comes with conversation. The first two, praxis and liturgy, often reflect subconscious theological affirmations that wash over us in the midst of our activities. The third purposeful engagement in reflection as a community is best done in a small coterie of like-minded searchers for truth and meaning. The seminar is the venue for this kind of activity

THEOLOGY AS ACTION (PRAXIS)

"Actions speak louder than words" is an old cliché. What we do reveals our commitments, although the basis of those commitments is not always apparent. Activity by itself is not a reflection, but it is reflective of our commitments. Those commitments, however, may not always be readily apparent. For instance, we may act to support a particular leader, but we may be acting out of a sense of survival rather than out of commitment to that leadership. Our commitment, then, is to survive, but that may not be evident to an outside observer.

We are doomed to repeat our mistakes when we do not reflect upon our actions. The reflective process that begins with our deeds is fundamental for successful adaptation to changing circumstances. It is also the basis for scientific studies as well as for discovering what is new. It provides a possibility of changing our behavior because we have learned from it. An action-based model of education helps people discover what they learn rather than be told what they ought to know, because it engenders a disciplined and nonjudgmental examination of what we do. To engage in this kind of reflection helps individuals to identify values and emphasize what they find worthy to pursue. I like to call this approach to education through discovery and reflection an "action/reflection" model of education.[2]

LITURGICAL ACTS

Liturgy is the work of the people in a worshiping community. The term "worship" is related to the word "worth." What we worship is what we find worthy of adoration, and the liturgy is the action of worship. Our liturgies, therefore, reveal what we find worthwhile to pursue. Our liturgical actions outline how we join a community, maintain it, celebrate it, and depart from it. For the community of the Church, the rituals that express these actions are baptism, confirmation, confession, the Eucharist, and celebration of special events such as weddings and the burial office. They reveal our belief in Christ and our love of God—what we find truly worthy of our adoration.

Our liturgy reflects what we find that is worthy of our attention. Other communities, such as the office staff or a club, have parallels when they organize welcomes for newcomers, occasional parties, outings or picnics, or farewells for those who are leaving the staff. The way we remember special moments reflects what we find worthy. All too often, however, the reflections we pursue in the wake of liturgical activities, if any, fail to help the learning process take place. That is why we need to create safe harbors or seminars in which reflection is safe.

---

2. See Bernard J. F. Lonergan, *Method in Theology* (New York: Seabury Press, 1972) 13ff. Lonergan suggests this approach, which he calls the "transcendental method." Its basic elements are experience, understanding, judging, and deciding. These are the steps of an action/reflection model of learning and discovery.

A seminar that pursues an action/reflection model as its orientation will develop its own liturgies. Those moments of worship are essential to sustain the seminar community in its reflection work. They set a tone and point to what is truly important. Liturgical moments as part of the seminar help to identify what is important, provide sustaining care, and celebrate occasions of wonder and joy.

The Seminar: An Arena for the Discovery of Meaning

Theological reflection may begin or grow out of meditation or academic inquiry. Yet ultimately, at least from a Christian point of view, it is a communal quest. A theology that is completely personal and fails to take others into account will inevitably fail. We were not conceived alone. We were not born alone. We cannot survive alone. We cannot enter the burial chamber alone. Each of these experiences is intensely personal, but each also requires the participation of others. This means that we must be concerned for others as we walk the road together. The seminar is a venue in which that reflective process may be engaged and in which we can find companions for a portion of the journey.

The theological meaning of our lives is a shared meaning, a shared quest, and a shared theology. God lives in our lives through the Church, through us who are part of the communion of all the saints. Our theological reflection takes on its life when it develops in community. Only when our theology takes shape as a shared vision does it have the opportunity to grow, to be checked against error, to be of use to others, and to become the defining ideas that outline what it is to be the Church.

DECIDING WHERE TO BEGIN

The quadri-polar model for theological reflection, which I describe more fully in subsequent chapters, offers four points of entry or poles into the reflection process: our activities, our tradition, our culture, and our beliefs.[3] Whenever a method is applied, it should be done with some thought about the outcome and with the knowledge that beginning at any one place will lead to the other poles. Each pole will provide some

---

3. This quadri-polar model is an interesting way to compose or critique a sermon. To be effective a sermon needs to focus on the theological tradition, but it requires a personal authenticity that can only come through the life and beliefs of the preacher. A sermon will have little impact unless it brings a larger meaning to the world around us, thus speaking to mundane events.

advantages and present some drawbacks. While it is possible to move from one pole to another, it is really not very helpful to try to focus on two poles at once. We can retain information and focus on another event, but it is virtually impossible to focus on an object and observe its motion at the same time without suffering from vertigo. The way to transcend the particularities of each pole is through metaphorical expressions. Those may be done verbally or by pictorial representations.

Learning takes place best when all four poles are engaged. That is to say, we learn when:

—we encounter new data (tradition);
—we are able to compare that information to what happens in the world (culture) around us;
—we are convinced that what we have learned is useful (belief);
—we are going to behave differently as a result (action).

For example: When we are taught to do simple mathematics, we do not know how to count until we know the numbers and how to use them. But that knowledge is not sufficient unless we are able to apply it. The decision to use our knowledge is an affirmation that we believe in its importance and value. In practical terms, knowledge of numbers and how to use them must translate into the practicality of maintaining a checkbook. The real demonstration of our knowledge resides in the ability to balance our accounts.

REFLECTION FROM EXPERIENCE

Focusing on something we have done, once we can take an opportunity to step back and reflect, makes it possible to create a very personal theology. It is possible to learn a great deal about ourselves and develop our theology as well as our moral stance if we can first distance ourselves from the event, then tell our story and find imagery that expresses it, so that we obtain a new perspective. Having both personalized and then objectified our story, we may then question it by bringing theological questions (what I call a theological interrogatory) to our image or metaphor.

Remember that it is difficult to focus on our own actions when an activity is still unfolding. In the heat of the moment, reflections tend to be self-justifying or even impossible because we rarely see beyond our own agenda.

Focusing on a personal event or activity may open up the possibility or even a call for change. It may be an interesting exercise, but the focus needs to remain on the personal if it is to make a difference. It does little good to focus on someone else's experience when that person is not part of the conversation. At best it is gossip, and at worst it becomes slander. In that case we are simply using someone else as a textbook case or as a surrogate. The call for personal reflection and its consequences are thus avoided, except as an afterthought.

METHODOLOGY

This examination of the relationship of the model for reflection and the types of discourse we may use to communicate and analyze life leads naturally to a more explicit consideration of how to go about this task. The model requires an analytical understanding of discourse types, but it does not provide methods. In other words, we are at the point of having examined the background, theory, and general design for an automobile. We have considered various levels of its components, from the basic elements to the sophisticated and specialized aspects. Next it is time to examine how to make the machinery work. We can now look at how the model may be put into action.

Theological Reflection
and the Seminar

The Purpose of the Seminar

The work of theological reflection as a community affair is best done in a small group or seminar consisting usually of six to twelve persons. To produce an effective seminar, the leader, guide, or mentor of a seminar needs to know how to organize it so that the conversation is guided. The goal is to achieve a dialogue that is free to explore nuances and paths of interest while retaining a sense of purpose and a destination.

To achieve a purpose two major elements need to be considered. First, the leaders need to know the essential elements of a seminar. This is something like knowing how to drive a car; it entails starting it, using the gears, the brakes, and the pedals, as well as possessing a map of the destination. It does not mean that every car—or in this case the seminar—has the various elements in the same place or that they all look alike, or even that the destination has been decided. In other words, every seminar will develop its own life and shape. Some will hum smoothly; others may be less sleek. All may encounter difficult periods and times of joy and wonder.

Second, the participants must know, or be guided through, a sequence of developments that proceed toward a conclusion while also permitting unexpected but interesting ideas to emerge. To pursue the analogy of the automobile, this is like knowing that the car will perform differently at different speeds and on different surfaces. The participants in a seminar need to discover that the emotional and intellectual nuances and tones in a seminar will vary as the life of the group develops. In other words, the seminar needs to "hang loose" with a "tight plan." The reflective process of a seminar may be described as a nonlogical operation. It has a pattern, but it no longer follows the static immutability of truth that comes from concentrating on finding what does not change (Plato and Aristotle) or on a dialectical progress within a closed system (Georg W. F. Hegel).[1]

The Necessary Elements of a Seminar

A successful seminar must include certain ingredients to become an effective learning venue. These are:

1. *Commitment.* A group of people motivated to work together and ready to share a degree of personal and professional openness is an essential ingredient. They must take responsibility for their life as a group rather than leave all decisions to a leader; however, the question of authority is complex, and participants bring varying expectations and orientations to the person in charge. Sharing authority means more than intellectual assent to having different individuals chair the meeting. Different from a coaching situation, it is virtually impossible to sustain commitment from participants in a seminar without sharing the leadership role.

2. *Leadership.* The leader of a seminar needs to assume the role of a mentor. An effective mentor knows that each participant shares in the responsibility of leadership and opens the gates for communications to occur. The mentor is a guide, not a lecturer or a director. To achieve the task of leading a seminar, a mentor must possess self-confidence, the ability to develop consensus in the group, and the ability to be vulnerable, open, and charitable about the thoughts and feelings of the participants.

The role of the seminar leadership requires someone to be an enabler rather than a provider of information and answers. The best description of a seminar leader is that, in lieu of being a director, he or she must become a mentor, someone who opens doors for others and then accompanies them on the journey.

A mentor does not need to be an expert in the discipline under consideration, but it is essential that she or he has an understanding of what is happening in the interaction of the group, the subject under discussion, and the learning cycle of a reflection process.

---

1. Bernard J. F. Lonergan, *Method in Theology* (New York: Seabury Press, 1972) 6. Lonergan is not writing about a seminar, but the new requirements to which he alerts his readers is that theology can no longer be assumed to exist as a static discipline. The seminar, I submit, needs to be designed to handle theological thinking as a nonlogical operation.

3. *Clarity about the task.* Students need to establish their purpose for gathering. They must schedule their work so that there is a clear beginning and a definite conclusion, and everyone involved knows what commitment to the group implies. While any program can have these guidelines, ultimately the participants must develop a consensus and set their own norms about their work. Conflicts in this area, especially over schedules, may reflect power struggles in the group that should be identified and discussed until a conclusion is reached.

4. *Time.* Participants must be willing to allocate at least two, probably three, hours per session so that there is sufficient time for interactions to develop. They need to be able to speak their minds. This requires "air time" and trust, especially if those who are reluctant or introverted are to find an opportunity to make their voices known.

5. *Size and participation.* A limit of at least five and no more than twelve participants will ensure sufficient interaction and preserve enough time for everyone to participate. Participants must also agree to be present at every session. When this is impossible, maintaining the relationship of the group requires that absent members inform the group about their absence. Trust will quickly evaporate if people drop in and out without explanation or regard for their fellow sojourners in a seminar. In this regard a seminar is like a pilgrimage, and all participants have their role to play, their ability to respond, and their personal quest.

6. *A shared discipline.* All participants share and participate in the study of a subject that is of common interest. All need not be and will not be equally knowledgeable, but each participant does bring his or her own unique experience, which deserves respect and adds to the learning experience. To expect everyone to know the same things about a given subject is a self-defeating ideal. In the interchange of information, however, knowledge increases for all. For Christians, the subject is God's self-revelation through the "Story of the People of God" as revealed in the Bible, the tradition, and the history of the Church. The lives of the participants in the seminar are the most recent and the most present experience of this continuing saga.

7. *Trust.* Trust is essential for a seminar to function. Communications occur on an emotional as well as an intellectual level when participants share their personal lives in an appropriate manner. Care must be taken not to ask participants to reveal more of their lives than they feel comfortable to offer, but the level of trust and the success of a group depends upon the degree that people can be open to one another. The

opposite of trust is living in anxiety and fear. Anxiety (unspecified fear) and fear narrow the area in which persons can communicate freely. These emotions make working in a seminar unproductive; they also reduce creativity, cooperation, and enthusiasm.

The leader of a seminar must encourage opportunities to develop the trust level, although often these precious moments occur spontaneously, in which case the mentor's task is similar to that of a midwife. The group will return periodically to the task of deepening the level of relationship and increasing interpersonal communications. Without self-disclosure communications and reflection are not possible, and the depth of the reflection depends upon the degree of open and free discourse that can be attained. The first step is to overcome free-flowing anxiety by identifying the fear behind it. Often when we identify our fears they disappear. Like demons, once named, their power is lost.

8. *Confidentiality.* Confidentiality is essential to protect the trust relationship. Confidentiality, however, does not mean secrecy, which can breed its own kind of anxious reaction. While participants should be free to talk about what they experience in a seminar, they should avoid revealing what others have shared or experienced. The rule of thumb is this: To tell your story is okay; to tell someone else's story is a breach of confidence. To tell about the process and the methods is okay. For more about this, see Chapter 15.

9. *Sharing experiences.* While there is a body of information to learn, the focus of the seminar should be on studying how that information affects our lives. To achieve this, participants must be willing to divulge something of their lives that embodies what they talk about. To share incidents, to hear from others how they experience similar situations, and to apply the information or experience related through the materials to their personal lives opens the arena of personal experience as a rich field for learning and discovery. Thus there develops a fourfold interplay between the participants lives, their beliefs, their culture, and the materials they are studying. This fourfold model of personal action, belief, tradition, and culture guides the path of discussion in seminars.

Telling our stories, however, is not always easy. We tend to editorialize and interpret rather than relate what has happened. Furthermore, we encounter the reality that any attempt to tell a story is already an interpretation. Participants in a seminar must learn to relate the information about what happened, who said or did what, and then to identify how they felt and what they thought. Being in touch with only our personal thoughts reduces the capacity to glean intuitive insights; being in touch with only our emotions produces a loss of direction and clarity. Insightful revelations emerge from our thoughts, our feelings, and our deeds.

10. *Generalizing on experience.* While direct discussion of the events of our lives is important, ultimately these must be generalized by the development of appropriate texts that become the property of the community or group. One important tool for this is the metaphor or image. Participants in a seminar must learn to develop ways of expressing their experiences in metaphorical or artistic terms that transcend their lives. Frequently, seeing life through imagery provides considerable illumination. Such symbols usually emerge from our stories because the power of a story is best conveyed by imagery.

Another way to generalize is to develop transcending statements, which are true for all participants yet point to the concrete example. Such statements usually contain two or more positive ideas that exist in tension, for only one idea can actually be pursued.

11. *Results.* While learning about our lives in relationship to a body of information is interesting, an additional element is also necessary to obtain a sense of satisfaction and completion. At some point the implications of what is learned need to be gleaned and affirmed or questioned. There is a payoff in the seminar when students acknowledge that they have learned something useful and then decide how to implement the benefits that have been gained.

12. *Social and religious interaction.* Every group develops certain rituals to mark important events. When a worshiping community gathers, this may be easily achieved because certain worship rites are known to everyone. Even when the seminar group is not of a religious nature, patterns to recognize significant moments evolve. Among them may be the desire to eat and drink together. Most groups will plan an occasional celebration or party and organize celebrations, rather than leaving to chance moments of greeting and separation, and recognizing special events in the lives of the participants, such as weddings, births of children, birthdays, illness, and deaths.

13. *Understanding group process.* Effective group leaders recognize that there is a pattern to group life from inception (birth) to closure (death). The leader must provide adequate means to permit the expression of the thoughts and feelings of the participants as various steps are encountered. Among the steps will be a period of dependency, challenges to the authority of the leader, stages of joy and celebration, and

moments of deep introspection followed by an appreciation for the power of the community that supports its participants. Sharing this analysis with the seminar group may assist group members to come to terms with behavior they did not understand. Coming after an experience that can serve as a teachable moment, this explanation can give legitimacy to what may have been difficult, because it reaffirms that times of conflict are an important and normal aspect of a group's development.

14. *Basic needs*. Finally, the group and the group leader must come to terms with the basic needs of any seminar group. These are threefold: (a) individual needs, (b) maintenance needs, and (c) task needs.

a) Individual needs are obvious, although they are sometimes disregarded. Personal comfort and needs usually require immediate attention. It is very difficult to concentrate on a discussion when one has severe personal needs such as hunger, thirst, bathroom needs, or uncomfortable accommodations. An effective seminar must take this a further step. It is important to ascertain and work out the group's life so that essential personal needs are met and everyone can participate fully. Some personal needs change, so this aspect must be reviewed regularly. The matter is complicated because we have social norms about acceptable personal needs, explainable personal needs, and personal needs that society does not perceive as genuine or acceptable.[2] These may differ in different settings.

b) Maintenance needs are about interpersonal relationships. They are often disregarded by groups and the leadership, who get caught up in personal agendas or in working out a task. This is why many groups fall apart.[3] To be effective, a seminar group needs to examine and discuss the interpersonal relationships from time to time. This may become intensely personal, but it is also part of the life of the group. When a group looks at its maintenance of group life it may wish to talk about why some are outspoken and others are silent, how group members relate

2. There are social norms that tend to govern how we express our needs. An example of an acceptable need is that of a comfortable place or seat. An explainable need is a request to be able to use a bathroom. An unacceptable need is a demand for permission to smoke in a place where smoking is not allowed.

3. A frequent experience in church and in society is that a meeting is called around a particular interest, and there is a big response. But subsequent sessions are sparsely attended, until finally the work is left to only a few. One of the most significant factors in this phenomenon is the failure to attend to maintaining the interpersonal relationship. Since people are not committed to one another, they abandon the community and the task ultimately flounders.

to each other, how decisions are made, how conflicts are handled, and examine the trust level which exists in the group. Jointly engaging in personality inventories that reveal how participants view and engage each other can be a very helpful and nonjudgmental tool. Some people are introverted, others extroverted. Some think first; others feel first. Some prefer structure and schedules; others are comfortable if matters float towards a conclusion. Knowing how we come to the seminar as persons can help everyone understand what is happening as well as bring out the best skills to the greater good of the learning community.

c) Every group has the need to have something to achieve, a task. The old saying "Idleness is the devil's workshop" has merit. If a task doesn't exist, the group will develop one, and therein is the possibility for mischief. But task needs also exist. Is it held in common? Is there consensus about the purpose? How will the group know when it is accomplished? What is the value of the enterprise? Do the end results justify the effort to be expended and the means to be employed?[4]

The Benefits of Seminars

A camel may look like an "animal which was put together by a committee," but when used appropriately a camel is a very efficient animal. It can carry its load, even when essential resources are low, over rough terrain and for long distances. The same may be said of seminars that allow participants to become invested in what they learn. Because they participate in the educational experience as part of the team, they have ownership and investment in both the process and the outcome. Indi-

---

4. Group members have roles to play in maintaining the function of their group and meeting individual, maintenance, and task needs. Individual needs are fulfilled by (1) possessing personal awareness; (2) owning one's position; (3) expressing personal thoughts and feelings; (4) deciding what to share; (5) leveling with others about what is going on internally; (6) confronting others as appropriate; (7) seeking clarification when something is not understood; (8) listening with care; (9) checking out what was heard and what has been communicated; (10) committing oneself to the work.

The maintenance needs are met by (1) encouraging; (2) being friendly and responsive; (3) expressing group feelings when these are recognized; (4) harmonizing or reconciling differences; (5) compromising; (6) admitting error; (7) gatekeeping (helping others to make their contributions); (8) setting standards.

Task needs are met by (1) initiating proposals; (2) seeking information and opinions; (3) providing information; (4) seeking clarification and explanations; (5) summarizing; (6) developing consensus.

viduals with different levels of knowledge, experience, motivation, and interest can work together effectively in the seminar context. Unlike other educational processes, which seek to mold each student to a given level of achievement, seminars allow participants to set their own goals and hold themselves accountable to their community rather than the demands of external standards authoritatively imposed.

All can learn from the experience of the lives of the participants. Everyone has experienced life, but each person has a different adventure so that both uniqueness and commonality exist among people in any learning community. Participants arrive as peers to the group and the learning process is a shared quest; thus the seminar becomes an exploration rather than a tedious task. While there may be difficult times, dry times, and hard times, participants in a seminar have the opportunity to discover and enjoy the excitement of learning.

Seminars work well for all ages, but they are especially appropriate for teaching mature adults who are best moved from personal motivations. In seminars individuals can set their own learning goals, they can learn from colleagues, and they can obtain help without being deemed or deeming themselves inadequate. In the climate of a small group, students can focus not only on the facts to be learned but also on the meaning of what they have imbibed so that they may be transformed by the experience.

Meditation: Internal Knowing

Our educational patterns teach us things from outside ourselves to internalize and apply to other situations. Traditional education programs do not usually include a component designed to help us examine our internal life as a place to learn. We tell people to "think" but fail to give space and provide time to meditate over what we have learned. Often we think that in-depth introspection is the domain of psychoanalysis and spirituality, something appropriate as a response to either psychological dysfunction or spiritual anguish. That is true when serious problems exist, but discovering one's internal life should really be part of our educational process. Spiritual reflection and analysis may thus be considered first as a learning method and secondarily as healing tools, although we frequently come to them first when in crisis.

Much may be learned through careful reflection, and our process of reflection can be greatly enhanced if it is guided by a capable leader. The sources of reflection are our thoughts, our emotions, our dreams, and our images as they emerge into consciousness in response to both internal and external stimuli. A seminar should provide opportunities for reflective thinking, silence, meditation, or quiet time. To make this most useful, we can also offer guidance about how to reflect by the use of personal journals (diaries), guided meditations, and methods of focusing our emotional and intellectual patterns through the reflective process.

The opportunity to reflect and to look inward is a very personal experience. It may be guided, and it may be pursued in groups on retreat. Discovering one's internal rhythms, thoughts, and feelings completes the learning process. Usually teachers discourage daydreaming, yet this can be a very important adjunct to learning, for this is the time to ponder and integrate what we have learned. Meditation, the opportunity to contemplate and appreciate, is an important aspect of the learning cycle, as is the exposition of our dreams. Indeed meditation and dreams are closely related, and both are important to the process of discovery. Good examples are the dreams of Joseph related in the Bible or the dream of August F. Kekule, who discovered the pattern for the benzene molecule in his reveries. Our dreams can provide visions that alter our perceptions of the world. This, too, is an important aspect of the educational process.

The Wonder of Discovery

The process of self-discovery can be a group or team effort. The seminar is a good arena in which to introduce patterns to help students reflect effectively. Looking inward or self-discovery is also a process of disclosing the unknown. Disciplined reflection may produce new knowledge or new ways to look at what we already know. The result is that our world changes in the process. Only through reflection do we begin to perceive and accept the shifts that mark a new world, a change in paradigms, a movement from one era to another.

The process of discovery may be the result of a systematic investigation, and it may happen in unpredictable ways through an unexpected insight, vision, or dream. Discovery may come through work in the laboratory, through scholarly study, and through inventions such as the computer, but what we know has no meaning until it is integrated into the fabric of our lives. All these describe learning processes in which the natural order teaches us something that we may then select to share with each other.

Discovery is the most energizing and miraculous part of the learning process. Whether someone is a scientist peering into the heavens, an explorer of unknown lands, or someone seeking to attain self-knowledge, discovery means that this individual has gone where others have not yet been and can now return to enrich others. The opportunity to discover is the opportunity to serve in its richest sense, for at that moment we share directly in the activity of creation. Whether in lectures, on the practice field, in a seminar or a deep, introspective trance, discovery is what makes learning a joy rather than a chore.

The Four-Source Model and Educational Methods

While the sources for a reflection are not fixed, we can identify certain elements or sources that are vital to a reflective process. These sources may be labeled Action, Tradition, Culture, and Belief. This model is a fundamental outline for the process of reflection. It is described much more completely in subsequent chapters.

The *Action Source* of the four-source model is that information which participants are willing to share and learn from in the reflection process. It comes from their lives. The *Tradition Source* is the information that we receive from the discipline under consideration, which in this case is theology. The *Culture Source* is that information we derive from other sources that impinges on our study, namely, what the world around us has to offer. The *Belief Source* pertains to the personal beliefs or affirmations (which may or may not be congruent with the actions) of those who are participating in the reflection process.

The four-source model clarifies the role of the four educational methods we have thus far reviewed: presentation, coaching, seminar, and meditation. A relationship that is not readily apparent exists between the two patterns (four sources and four methods). That relationship suggests what methods to emphasize when offering a particular educational opportunity. In any educational enterprise, like theological reflection, all four methods are always present, but usually one is emphasized while the others are on the sidelines.

Each educational method tends to favor growth and learning in three of the four sources. In each case the fourth source is the subject of indirect rather than direct focus. It exists and grows in the shadow while the group focuses clearly on the other three sources.

Presentations and the Four-Source Model

From a presentation we may learn new information and encounter ideas that test, challenge, or form our beliefs. What is not touched directly is our experience or activity. Since students are passive (taking notes is an aid to retaining information, but basically a passive or receptive attitude), they are recipients of the educational process.

When one moves from lecturing to an activity such as a laboratory experiment, the educational method shifts to another stage. Action here is a shadow side to the presentation or lecture rather than the immediate activity of the lecture.

Coaching and the Four-Source Model

Coaching or on-the-job training involves the three primary areas of tradition, action, and culture. When being coached, a student must (1) learn the culture that accompanies the skill. This usually includes (2) a tradition formulated in the jargon or "in" language, the nonverbal behavior, and the attire for the (3) activity under consideration. A student must develop an appreciation of the tradition that supports that culture and must learn and practice appropriate exercises. Beliefs or personal positions fall in the shadows when we are coached to learn an activity. Coaching is action-oriented, and beliefs are secondary. Doing is what counts, and that means success with the activity, passing the examination, winning the game, or becoming a virtuoso. After students learn the activity, the belief system emerges from the shadows as the activity fills the life of the participant.

The Seminar and the Four-Source Model

The seminar emphasizes the opportunity to offer reports of (1) personal activities, brings to scrutiny (2) a common tradition, and offers (3) a setting for expressing beliefs. The seminar is not a good place to resolve issues pertaining to culture, because it is very difficult to identify the cultures from which we speak when we are working in a seminar. Within the seminar setting, the cultures we inhabit are often in the shadow, hard to pin down, and elusive. In that venue information from the culture tends to become "straw figures" to which we attach what we think is wrong with the world.

Seminars offer an area in which we may develop our sense of meaning about what we do, learn, and believe. The seminar provides an opportunity for exploration, discussion, and making decisions from what emerges. It leads naturally to reflection, and often the result is that a new culture develops, first in micro-form, as people who develop the language of a particular small group, and then in macro-form, when a sufficiently large group of people share the same vision. When we have a sense of meaning in our lives, this informs all our activities and becomes part of our culture, albeit a culture somewhat transformed.

Meditation and the Four-Source Model

Meditation and reflection may be done alone, under guidance, or as part of a group, but here the emphasis is on introspection and self-analysis. Often seminars employ this kind of activity. Meditative/reflective activities examine (1) our beliefs, ponder (2) what we have done (activity), and look at (3) our relationships with one another within the culture(s) we inhabit. But when we meditate, it may become difficult to focus on the disciplined study of tradition, since the meditation itself requires a focus on a particular tradition.[5] Too much data overwhelms a reflection; thus tradition, data, and scientific analysis are relegated to the shadows when we meditate.

Care must be taken not to let meditation become the only core for our spontaneity; that might launch us into enthusiastic fervor that becomes our only spiritual quest. When spirituality loses contact with data and we presume that the culture must be converted rather than engaged, there arises an anti-intellectual or anti-social bias. The basis of this notion is that scholarly studies and scientific critiques destroy the enthusiastic spirit. Rather than being an end in itself, meditation should lead us out of the shadows to spirituality, a new search for data and extrinsic reality. Spirituality is more than being filled with fervor. It contains the totality of human experience—passion, reason, and activity. If we act without passion and reason, we are robots. If we act without passion, we lack energy. If we act without reason, we become dangerous fools.

---

5. Two methods of reflection that are analytical but not purely meditative are those offered by Clinical Pastoral Education (CPE) and the Case Study method. Both have difficulty when addressing Christian tradition, which always lurks in the background as an underlying assumption. While they are reflective and analytic, neither easily uses a vehicle for making the transcendental connection. This is where metaphors or images have a role. According to the Whiteheads, "Weaknesses sometimes experienced in both methods are a paucity of explicit attention given to the Christian Tradition . . . and a difficulty of moving from . . . concrete incidents to broader theological understanding." James D. Whitehead and Evelyn Eaton Whitehead, *Method in Ministry: Theological Reflection and Christian Ministry* (San Francisco: Harper & Row, 1980) 5. Using the seminar as an arena where participants may search for the transcendent factors by developing appropriate "stories" is to offer the analytical disciplines a path by which to connect itself to historical and scientific roots.

Meditation is best used to focus on the inner self or on discovering what is truly new and can then be shared with others. Since meditation depends upon new insights to develop, it is the most exciting and the most risky learning enterprise. It is also the source from which a new history or tradition is built.

Integrating Educational Methods with a Model of Theological Reflection

We have seen the four-source model (tradition, culture, belief, and action) and how this may describe how four educational methods (action, tradition, culture, belief) interact. This is a model of "theological" reflection, but it becomes theological only when one employs a theological mode of interrogation.[6]

The model of theological reflection is first a model for learning, one that suggests numerous methods, applications, and possibilities. The key factor is finding the appropriate questions that represent the discipline under consideration and bringing to the work the tradition or body of knowledge applicable to that enterprise. In many cases the body of knowledge for various disciplines will be more or less the same, but the questions asked will make the difference. To develop theological questions, we must possess a set of questions that explore the sources so as to evoke useful answers. I call this most important and difficult task that of developing a theological interrogatory.

Developing the Transcendent: The Use of Metaphor[7]

Metaphors are the building blocks of larger stories or myths. Those stories provide texts that transcend our mundane experiences. Through metaphors we reach beyond ourselves and develop the formative stories that are our mythologies. In turn our myths bring understanding to our experience. By transcending our experience we return affirmed, renewed, enlightened, and transformed. We touch the lore of the past, energize the present, and look prospectively to the future.

6. Other disciplines bring their own interrogatories. One could see sets of questions emerging from law, medicine, sociology, psychology, anthropology, history, etc.

7. I do not engage in the differentiation between simile and metaphor, which is a technical one. What matters here is that we develop imagery rather than the technicality of whether "like" or "as" is used in the statement that establishes a metaphorical image. This is not to degrade the literary discipline but simply to emphasize what matters here.

The first step is discovery. The second step is to teach others about the discovery. Conveying the lore to others acts as a test of our knowledge as well as a review. One usually cannot convey to others what one has not truly learned. Often we learn clearly only when we are called to teach others and guide them through their own process of discovery. Education as discovery or sharing what we know is much more exciting than being a recipient. When we learn something new, we participate in the creative process rather than becoming consumers of what others have done. Any new discovery has a startling or surprising element. We may view what we find with joy or dismay, but there is always excitement, even if that excitation is borne on the wings of terror rather than those of ecstasy. The excitement comes because we know that we are in the midst of profound change, of death and of birth.

Encouraging the use of metaphors is one way to bring the discovery process to education. Metaphors help us to transcend and rise beyond the important yet petit events of daily life. Whether we are using a lecture, coaching, or a seminar, metaphors can serve to enhance the process of discovery. The result is that knowledge increases in depth, content, and utility. Through the imagery of metaphors we become participants in the learning process rather than remaining passive recipients. We become explorers who delight in being able to shout "Eureka!" ("I have found it!").

PART III

Theological Reflection

Methodology, Leadership, and Consequences

CHAPTER 11

Sources for Theological Reflection

Historical Notes

Identifying the sources of theology is not a new venture. In the six-teenth century Melchior Cano, a Spanish Dominican, developed a sys-tematic presentation in which he outlined ten sources. These were:

1) Scripture;
2) The tradition of Christ and the apostles;
3) The authority of the Catholic Church;
4) The councils, especially the general councils;
5) The authority of the Roman Church;
6) The authority of the Fathers;
7) The authority of scholastic theologians;
8) Natural reason;
9) The philosophers and jurists;
10) History.[1]

Within Anglicanism, one of the most celebrated statements about the sources of theology is the statement attributed to Richard Hooker,[2] who allegedly suggested that the sources of faith are Tradition, Scrip-ture, and Reason.[3] This point of view has long dominated Anglicanism

1. Melchior Cano, *De locis theologicis libri duodecim* (Salamanca, 1563). Cited in Raymond F. Collins, *Models of Theological Reflection* (Boston: University Press of America, 1984) 38–39.
2. This seventeenth-century theologian did not evoke the three sources as clearly as his apologists sometimes suggest. He has been interpreted in this way, however, and the three-source model has become an accepted feature of Anglican theology. Some further refined the three sources by suggesting that reason is rooted in experience. Methodists tend to make experience a fourth source.
3. More recently some involved in renewal movements have used a

as a counterpoint to Rome and evangelical Protestants. The former looked to the authority of the *magisterium* or authority of the Church, tradition, and the Bible; the latter tended to insist that all faith comes only from the biblical Scriptures *(biblia sola)*.

More recently David Tracy suggested a two-source model for theology: the texts of the Christian tradition and the language and experience common to all human beings.[4] Anglican theologian John Booty combined Hooker and Tracy by suggesting that the sources are Scripture, tradition, reason, and experience, which interweave and sometimes seem to fly apart.[5]

A Three-Source Model

In 1980 James and Evelyn Whitehead published a three-source model for reflection that has been very influential among Christian educators. It describes a pattern for theological reflection on ministry.[6] Their triangular schema has three poles: tradition, culture, and personal experience. Tradition is defined as "pluriform in Scripture and history." Personal experience is what the individual believer and the community bring to the reflection. Cultural information is data from the culture that influence the issue in question.

The Whiteheads focused on the professional concerns of the minister, particularly the examination of the pastoral relationship. They sought to broaden the analysis made possible through the case-study method and verbatims used in Clinical Pastoral Education (CPE). They also described a method to apply their model. Their method has three overlapping stages:

1. *Attending:* Seek out the information on a particular concern that is available in personal experience, Christian tradition, and cultural sources.

2. *Assertion:* Engage the information from these three sources in a process of mutual clarification and challenge in order to expand and deepen religious insight.

---

three-legged stool as a model for the sources of theology. The three legs are the Bible, tradition, and experience.

4. David Tracy, *Blessed Rage for Order: The New Pluralism in Theology* (New York: Seabury Press, 1978) 43–44.

5. John E. Booty, *What Makes Us Episcopalians?* (Wilton, Conn.: Morehouse-Barlow, 1982) 2.

6. James D. Whitehead and Evelyn Eaton Whitehead, *Method in Ministry: Theological Reflection and Christian Ministry* (San Francisco: Harper & Row, 1980) 11ff.

3. *Decision:* Move from insight through decision to concrete pastoral action.[7]

The Whiteheads developed their model a step further. They suggested that theological reflection can investigate the relationship of the poles represented by tradition and cultural information. The investigation of the tradition and culture provided the "theoretical" aspect. "Secular reflection" linked the poles representing cultural information and personal experience. A "fundamentalist reflection" connected the poles of tradition and personal experience.[8] Reflection on ministry required the examination of all three links—theoretical, fundamentalist, and secular.

The Four-Source Model

Under the influence of its founder, Charles L. Winters, and its first full-time trainer, Flower Ross, the Education for Ministry program began with a three-source model.[9] But this differed from that of the Whiteheads in that the three sources were (1) tradition, (2) experience or action, and (3) position or belief (which included an individual's cultural perspective. John de Beer and Patricia O. Killen added an element in 1982–83 by separating culture from personal beliefs and position, so that a four-source model emerged.

The four-source model was used to develop methods for seminars in support of theological education by extension. Unlike the Whiteheads, who suggested that the reflection had the primary purpose of helping with the professional/pastoral task, EFM used the four-source model to make theological sense of all life experiences. This was rooted in the notion that ministry occurs in every human activity. What is at stake is

7. Ibid., 22. This three-stage process of intervention has echoes in the field of medicine and the nature of the relationship between the patient and the physician, who is in attendance.

8. Ibid., 97.

9. EFM's four-source model represents the distillation of the work of many people who were acquainted with these works and participated in the development of the EFM program. Principals involved in the development of the four-source model were Charles L. Winters, originator of the EFM program; his associate, Flower Ross; and about seventy trainers for EFM located in the United States, New Zealand, Canada, Australia, the Bahamas, Central America, and Europe. Because of its ongoing training and dialogue with trainers, mentors, and students, many of its methods and models truly are communal. While a few individuals had great impact on the program's developments, thousands can rightfully claim a share in it too.

our perception of the activity and how we enter into it. If God is omnipresent, then God's work is too, and from that analogy one may begin to see that ministry is always present as well. Sometimes we are not sensitive to it, and often we do it badly, but the opportunity is there.

The four sources used by the Education for Ministry program are: (1) Christian tradition (Bible, liturgy, and history); (2) human experience or activity; (3) beliefs or positions; (4) culture. The key element that made the reflective process theological, however, was the dimension of a theological interrogative. It became Christian theology when that interrogatory and the tradition came from the Christian classics. In this quadri-polar model each source might be examined by various interrogatives, and so it has interdisciplinary teaching potential. Among those dedicated to the ministry of the Church, theology is the appropriate subject to pursue. Nevertheless, other interrogatories could also be brought to the topic under scrutiny.[10]

Making Sense of the Sources

Two sources, three sources, four sources—how best to make sense of this? Perhaps a useful way to approach the problem is to first recognize what has plagued Western thought, namely, a division between the self and that which is outside oneself. This is a dualism that finds multiple expressions in theology—Church and society, personal faith versus the Church's faith, to name only two as examples. To reflect theologically requires that we identify with precision what we are to examine, to do this in a variety of ways, and then to make comparisons, draw contrasts, and seek congruence as well as differences. Thus our sources break down into two general areas: that which is personal and intrinsic to the self and that which is exterior to the self. The personal and intrinsic further divides into what we do and what we believe. What is exterior to our personal experience has loosely been labeled as culture. In reality, of course, we are speaking of the world around us, which we know through human culture and through natural events. Because we are focused on

10. The four-source model is a model that may be used to express the application of various teaching methods. This has been done at such varied locations as Texas A & M to teach rural sociology, Auburn University to teach educators, and the Medical College of Georgia to work and teach those working with persons who suffer long-term chronic diseases. The reflection model of education tends to allow individuals to make changes of their own volition and at their own pace. That brings about a successful adaptation to their chronic situation.

one particular aspect of culture, the tradition of our Christian faith, this has been extrapolated.[11]

How to Use the Personal Sources

EXPERIENCE OR ACTION

Understanding the complexities of human experience is often best accomplished through stories. We tell what happened, who was there, when and where it took place, and what affected the activity we describe under the rubric of "experience."[12] Reflection on experience is always a reflection on history, but it is usually a personal rather than a corporate history. Even in a group that has experienced something together, the individual experience and interpretation of people in the same group will differ significantly.

Human experience worthy of theological reflection may be as cataclysmic as occasions of birth, marriage, illness, and death. Occasions of no apparent import can serve equally well. All experience counts as significant even if it is something as mundane as an interaction while washing dishes or a chance encounter with an old friend. Theology emerges from the

---

11. I would note at this juncture that the reflective methods we present can be used to examine non-Christian traditions or even other disciplines. In such a case, what would be extrapolated from the culture would be the faith or discipline under study.

12. James Griffis, "The Dialectic of Experience," unpublished paper presented to the Conference of Anglican Theologians, W. Cornwall, Connecticut, September 22, 1994. Griffis examines the use of this notion in contemporary theology. It is not popular with those who emphasize the Bible as the source of theology, since an emphasis on "experience" would suggest a devaluation of the biblical message. But there are other critiques to promulgate. The naive use of "experience" occurs when the term covers such a far-reaching set of circumstances that the term reveals too little about too much. There is also an uncritical use of experience that fails to note the relationship of the knowing subject and the object of the knowledge. Finally, there exists the mistaken notion that experience is primarily a mental process or that we know faith from experience. What we offer here is a method to approach working with theology that begins in experience clearly and narrowly defined so that it may be examined closely. A careful examination of human experience differentiates between the event itself and the thoughts and feelings associated with the experience. Physiologically we seek to examine the experience in terms of the physical activity involved. But this can only be done in rational (cerebral) terms and emotive (limbic) processes. All three—the act, the thought, and the emotive—are part of the analysis needed to develop a congruent reflection.

common experiences of our lives. Reflection need not be relegated only to the dramatic or the tragic. The mundane and joyous moments serve just as well as occasions upon which we may reflect and learn to think theologically.

Identifying an experience can be uncomfortable. Telling a story and exploring the thoughts and feelings encountered during a particular event may reveal more than we are comfortable showing. It may also reveal discontinuity between what we do and what we believe; however, for those who seek a deeper understanding and meaning in their lives, the risk is worth it, since the returns are abundant.

BELIEFS AND OPINIONS

Beliefs come from many sources. We accept many things as truth because someone in authority has informed us. Indeed, a society becomes chaotic and self-destructive without a set of beliefs accepted by most of the people. This is the social contract that binds us into a community. We are unable to verify everything we learn, so our existence depends upon our acceptance of a usable system of beliefs. Of course, this says nothing about whether the belief is right or wrong (morally), correct or fallacious (factually). It is inevitable that beliefs and opinions tend, at least to some degree, to be prejudgments and, therefore, *de facto* prejudicial.

When we hold a belief, we assume that it is right and correct, or else it does not qualify as a belief. It expresses a position we have taken and are willing to defend. Those beliefs are important and precious to us because our worldview must change significantly should we be forced to give up or alter a fundamental position or belief. Our positions are the exterior faces of the internal paradigms that form and inform our lives. They are essential to life and very difficult to examine, alter, or give up without conflict.

Many beliefs, of course, are learned early, only to be challenged later. Some beliefs develop because we misinterpret what we see. Others develop because we knowingly or unconsciously mislead ourselves or because others purposely mislead us, such as telling children the legend of Santa Claus. There is something important about the expression "Seeing is believing." It is easy to fool the eye, as a sleight-of-hand artist can demonstrate, and so it is also easy to fool the mind. Sometimes beliefs are just a set of prejudices based on fears or lifelong indoctrination. But beliefs are also formed and sustained by social pressures. For instance, someone who believes that the Bible contains the literal words of God will not fare well in a liberal university society. On the other hand, a scientifically trained scholar will not be very appreciated in a pre-scientific culture still intent on a hand-to-mouth existence. Many social conflicts occur because beliefs are in conflict, perhaps even antithetical; however, usually the conflicts do not arise until the belief is put into action, or at least the existence of a presumption of a threat that such action is imminent. That is when cultural values clash and conflict becomes inevitable.

One caveat about reflecting on a person's beliefs needs to be added. The beliefs we hold are often very special and precious. They can be the occasion for great debates, but debate and reflection are not the same thing. A debate may, however, become the experiential fodder for future reflection. In a debate each side expects to fight for its position, perhaps even appeal it to a higher authority if an unfavorable decision occurs as the result of a debate.[13] When reflection occurs, we are not seeking a winner or a loser in the classical sense of a debate; we are offering an opportunity for discovery and concern for change.

How to Use the External Sources

THE TRADITION[14]

Within the context of Christian theology, the tradition encompasses the Bible or Holy Scripture, Church history, and what may best be defined as the Church's position. Thus the exploration of the Christian tradition in an Anglican way encompasses both Roman Catholic and Protestant perspectives. This is an immense corpus of material, and a key to its use is the selection of the materials to be considered at any given moment as the featured text for a reflective focus.

Holy Scripture usually refers to the Bible, although precisely what we should include to form the biblical text differs for various Christian bodies. Within the scope of theological reflection, the canon of Scripture may be somewhat open-ended. Historical documents of the biblical era that do not fit in the canon are, of course, included with history.

---

13. For instance, public debates occur regularly as part of the legislative processes. The laws that result may may in turn be overturned by the courts.

14. The Whiteheads' description of tradition as pluriform needs expansion *(Method in Ministry, 196)*, as does the description in Patricia O'Connell Killen and John de Beer, *The Art of Theological Reflection* (New York: Crossroad, 1994) 55. Killen and de Beer provide a useful description of tradition but do not respond to the question: Who decides what is useful tradition?

History, even when taught in a theological setting, contains more than just institutional Church or religious history; it also includes the secular factors that have surrounded the history of religion. Even when Church and state are legally separate, they still coexist on the same turf. They possess the same relative constituency and are influenced by the ebb and flow of the same issues of war, peace, famine, illness, natural disasters, and technological change. Secular and ecclesiastical histories, therefore, are inexorably linked as part of our tradition. Scholars often perceive secular concerns in the midst of ecclesiastical conflicts, and faithful people in turn claim that God's grace exists in the midst of secular events.

In some circles the magisterium refers to the authority of the Church. If it is understood in the creative rather than the authoritarian sense, a whole other and important dimension of tradition emerges. The magisterium can refer to the eschatological triumph,[15] the existence of Christ in and through the Church. The *ecclesia,* or Church, represents the messianic presence, the divine unity, the *anamnesis* (recollection), and the power of God in Christ, not only by its history but by its ongoing presence and achievements. Thus the magisterium represents the Church as the incorporation of the people of God doing God's work today.

The magisterium in non-Latin tradition is somewhat more than, but not relatively different from, the authority of the Church's decisions and pronouncements. Only those Church groups whose polity lacks any sense of national identity and emphasizes only the local congregation fail to have some sense of the authority and responsibility of the larger community.

CULTURE

We live in many cultures with ethnic, economic, educational, linguistic, racial, and religious diversities. Our cultures harbor political, religious, and professional distinctions as well as sexual and age differences. The difference between the culture of the surgeon and that of the butcher is significant, even though they have similar interests—knives and anatomy. Each has its own activities and language. Language differences are always important because language gives formative shape to a culture. Our media of communications affect our messages and at their roots always have a set of metaphors or symbols that we use to evoke our experience.

15. Karl Rahner, "Magisterium," in *Encyclopedia of Theology*, ed. Karl Rahner (New York: Seabury Press, 1975) 872.

Since we evoke our cultures in language, the symbols emerge from our experience and beliefs. Our belief systems reflect our own conclusions, but they also reflect our cultures. There is a bipolarity to the notion of culture. On one side is the culture in which we live. It can be so much part of our lives that we are unable to differentiate between what we developed internally and what we acquired from our society. On the other side are those aspects of culture from which we separate ourselves or which we do not assume as belonging to us. We may say, then, that we live in a Western culture and identify quite clearly that this is very different from an African, Native American, Hispanic, or Asian culture, even though elements of these cultures exist in ours.

The twentieth century has been an era when cultures have encountered one another with a frequency and impact never before experienced. We have become much more accepting and cognizant of other cultures as well as more resentful of the alien and defensive of our own affirmations. Nevertheless, we are overwhelmed by a plethora of disjunctive cultural signals. We can drive down a major street of any town and observe restaurants that belong to cultures as diverse as those of China, Indonesia, Argentina, and France. Television assaults us with news and pictures from throughout the world, and we adopt mores and customs from throughout the world if they seem to fit our needs. Music and theater from throughout the world are available to us on local stages and through the electronic media. So while we encounter many cultures, we also tend to blend together some of what we obtain from many corners of the world, and it may be said that we have become a global community and a global culture.

Norms, habits, language, and expectations differ from profession to profession, from job to job, even from company to company working in the same field. Jargon is always a sign of a specific culture or subculture. Jargon serves as linguistic shortcuts. But it also excludes those who do not know the jargon, for it creates a subculture that excludes those who are not able to access the special lingo.[16]

The culture of the *ecclesia*, or Church, however, is more complex than that of being one among many. The faith of our ancestors, translated, passed on, shared, and adapted, imbues our various cultures. It is

---

16. The computer world has become a prime example of this phenomenon, but it really applies to every subgroup that forms a special interest around work, pleasure, political cause, or social grouping.

not possible to separate what comes as cultural baggage and what comes as Church history and tradition. For instance, we encounter real confusion about Christmas, which began as a christianized pagan feast to celebrate the winter solstice. Today it suffers from a cultural emphasis because of the commercial concerns that now surround this feast day, which was once largely religious.

Culture leads us back to the tradition of our faith. The model we have been using really contains a series of polarities between each of the four points, which may be connected like a quadrilateral pyramid.

Learning Methods: A Quadripolar Model

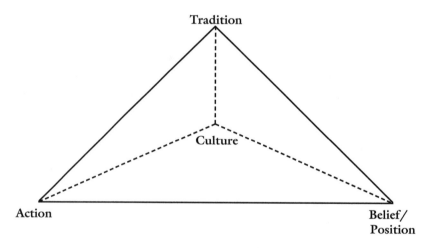

ATB—The Seminar Method (Culture)
ACT—Coaching (Belief)
BCT—Lecture/Presentation (Action)
ACB—Spiritual Direction/Analysis (Tradition)

Each face represents an educational methodology. The point opposite each triangular face represents an aspect under development. The developing aspect is difficult to examine. For example, a student must wait to engage in an activity until the presentation or lecture is concluded. When coaching, the focus is on the activity being taught and its context. Beliefs must often be suspended when trying out new activities. Finally, when engaged in a seminar, it often becomes very difficult to identify the culture and examine it without bringing in personal experience and beliefs or judgments about it.

Such a model may be useful to suggest connections and relationships. It must not be seen, however, as anything more than a useful way to view the relationships of different aspects of our theological experience.

The four sources or poles may be visualized as points on a four-sided pyramid. But they are also like the threads of a single piece of cloth. The boundaries are not distinct. Some may say that they are clearly at one point or another in the model, but they can never be certain exactly where the crossing place exists. The movement through the four-source model is best described as a nonlinear process rather than a static description.

The four poles are useful as demarcations to describe our existence and its relationship to the universe. To deal with reality, we always have to consider something of its aspects. To focus our attention, we select a focus from one or two of the poles in order to achieve clarity. Reflection thus requires a process of selection and exclusion in order to clarify, analyze, and draw implications. It is a constant movement from broad considerations to the narrow, and then back to the broad as we generalize what we have learned from the particular.

THEOLOGICAL REFLECTION AND THE FOUR SOURCES

Everyone reflects to some degree or another. Experience really is whatever happens to us, and we all think about what happens to us. What makes a particular reflection theological, and what makes it Christian theology? Answering that question is the key to understanding the difference between using a method to learn theology and using that method to learn another discipline.

When we think about events and ask if they were good or bad, legal or illicit, fair or prejudicial, we are reflecting, but not just as theologians. We begin the theological questions when we begin to ask about the meaning of events and seek to find something that transcends or goes beyond the existential. At that point we have begun the step of looking to God. The answers we derive may then inform our ethical and practical concerns. The first aspect of what makes theological reflection is that it points us, through life, to seek God in the questions as well as the answers.

Finding meaning, of course, does not mean that we are theist. Even the atheist, and certainly the agnostic, has a way of finding meaning. Taking the next step in a Christian context, seeking God and making our reflection Christian go together as one leap, the leap of accepting that God's love exists.[17] In a fallen world we may then come to discover that love transcends and that it must be known in creation as a divine gift. When we ask questions that seek to find that divine gift and associate the work of Jesus Christ as the chief focus of that gift, we have leapt from searching for meaning to searching for the meaning of the Messiah in our lives. Our reflection has become a developing Christian theology.

17. The leap from faith in God to the affirmation of particular religion is, quite obviously, not always a leap to Christianity. Christians can affirm, however, that whenever the love of God is present, regardless of the religion being practiced, an element of Christianity is also present.

CHAPTER 12

Methods and Techniques

A Skill to Be Learned

Theological reflection is a skill to be learned. To learn any skill, like riding a bicycle or flying an airplane, requires coaching and hands-on practice as well as information. The same is true for learning to engage in theological reflection as well as a secondary skill, namely, learning how to teach others to engage in theological reflection.

In earlier chapters I identified sources for theological reflection and some of the problems inherent in language and types of discourse. This chapter presents methods and techniques for theological reflection. Ultimately those are learned best in workshops in which future guides or mentors for reflection can develop their skills. With that caveat, what follows is a general description of methods that may prove more useful to someone who has been working with this than to someone who arrives at this information for the first time. Specific applications are in the Appendices (pp. 195–213).

Prerequisites for Theological Reflection

A theological reflection is a guided conversation. It has a life of its own, and, like life, it usually follows a generally predictable progression from beginning to end. While the timing of any phase of a group's life cannot be precisely predicted, a group eventually passes through various phases from dependency and friendship, through conflicts, and into resolution and discovery of new opportunities. At the end of this chapter is a list of "What to do if . . .," which provides suggestions for conversations that cannot be taken through every step of a reflection because of insufficient time.[1]

---

1. Of course, a conversation can be aborted or curtailed. A conversation is usually aborted when the participants become fearful or the conversation does

129

Elements of Theological Reflection

GATHERING THE LEARNING COMMUNITY AND DEVELOPING TRUST

The way we gather is fundamental. If it develops anxiety, the work of reflection will be inhibited from the beginning. If the community develops a climate of warmth and support amidst diversity, the reflective process will thrive and be productive. Learning can best take place when we feel energized and hence are somewhat intense but in a supportive atmosphere. A learning opportunity, even a painful one, develops best in a safe and caring environment.

SETTING THE STAGE

We are accustomed to arriving at a meeting, introducing ourselves, perhaps adding whom or what we represent and from where we came. That kind of self-introduction is the socially acceptable way of "breaking the ice" and the first step to developing trust. In a seminar that will delve deeply into theological reflection on the basis of the lives of the participants, more is required to develop that sense of community that allows them to feel free to share some of their heartfelt ideas.

The art of storytelling returns once again as an important method by which to develop that trusting community. In this case it is the personal story that needs to be shared. A recounting of appropriate biographical events can quickly break barriers and overcome the isolation that exists between people who do not know one another. This is not a process that can be pressed. It is up to each individual to decide how much to share, but the more complete and personal the sharing, the greater the trust that will develop. What is most important, however, is authenticity. To share highly sensational aspects of one's life can just be one-upmanship. What best conveys our trust to others is the authenticity of our emotions and the clarity of our story, one rendered without remorse or blame.

There are some simple techniques for organizing a spiritual autobiography. One is to relate it in fifteen-year increments. Another is to describe a picture, which can act like a snapshot, of various stages of one's life. Still another is to share something about the relationships one has

---

not meet their needs. Changing the subject or experiencing some participants becoming silent may be symptoms of an aborted conversation. To curtail a reflection on purpose is a decision to be made by the group or its leadership, perhaps because the topic is inappropriate or because there is insufficient time to continue.

enjoyed with the people who were most significant in his or her life. And still another may be to share one's hobbies or to talk about tangible items that serve as signposts along the way, for instance, a pocketknife acquired when scouting or a license plate from one's first automobile. Most people usually have a box full of such treasures that can serve as talismans of the past.

MAINTAINING THE STAGE

Once a seminar begins, each time it gathers it is very helpful to catch up on relationships by allowing each participant to express what he or she would like to share concerning the time since the last meeting. This onboard time, as well as sharing stories during the course of the reflection process itself, serves to bond the group in a community of concern.

DECIDING ON A METHOD TO FOLLOW

Reflection does not just happen, even when it seems to be no more than a wonderful conversation. Certain elements need to be present in any method. They are more or less the same as the necessary elements of any productive conversation. Once trust exists, agreement about the topic is essential. This means that someone must initiate the topic with a personal story or with information upon which the conversation can focus. That topic must be sufficiently global to be of interest to everyone present and yet also be perceived to have a personal significance. In other words, the topic must be at once universal and personal.

It is important to be specific. Reflections or conversations that are truly non-specific or that flit from one topic to another without links quickly become very dull and a means of avoidance or a filibuster. When this pattern recurs frequently, it probably masks a desire to avoid tension and the painful reality of mistrust. It has to be confronted to be overcome, for it is like a demonic force that cannot be tamed until it is named.

To learn about a specific topic is one thing; to learn its meaning is something else. Often insights can be gathered from the conversation or reflection that lead to someone saying, "This is like . . ." While this is not technically a metaphor, such an utterance does lead the conversation from the specific data to an image that bridges the contribution of each individual in the conversation and yet provides some distance from the initial event and its presentation. As we have seen, the role of metaphors is to "bear across" or bridge across.

A satisfying reflection makes use of the expertise that is available. There is something to be learned, and it is all the more satisfying when those who participate can express their feelings and admit to what they have learned. A reflection also may take into consideration other relevant information, such as what various cultural elements bring to the discussion.

RECAPPING THE ESSENTIAL ELEMENTS

The following steps highlight the major elements of a reflective conversation:

1. Focusing on a significant topic.
    a) Someone offers a topic or relates a personal event.
    b) The participants in the seminar identify particulars in the topic that evoke energy for the reflection.
    c) Participants identify for themselves and the group where that energy touches their lives.

2. Focus on the core element.
    a) Develop an image or metaphor that expresses the core element(s) of the topic under consideration, or
    b) Develop a verbal statement that expresses the core element(s) of the topic.

Analysis

3. Explore the image, metaphor, or statement according to the rules of the discipline being used. In the case of theological reflection, ask classical theological questions. Some are suggested in the next chapter. Asking questions so as to promote learning and discovery is one of the most difficult tasks a mentor must accomplish. It is, however, essential to the learning process. How we phrase a question makes a difference and tends to predict the answer.

External Considerations

4. Now comes the time to bring other factors and disciplines into the discussion.
    a) What does the tradition or discipline under consideration bring to the discussion? In a theological reflection the theological tradition to be considered may be very expansive. As I have noted

earlier, among Christians there exist different expectations about the sources for theology, although all begin with the biblical message. Some Christians include the authority of the Church and the Church's theological and historical traditions as sources for theology, while others affirm that faith comes only from the Bible.

b) What does our knowledge of the world bring to the discussion? This needs to be focused on some accessible and commonly shared aspects of people's experience. Often it may come from a particular area of the wider culture. It is often necessary to focus on a certain element of culture, such as television, the news media, architecture, or politics.

Conversation

5. Now it is time to converse. How do the various sources impinge on the topic under review? Where does support exist? Where do we find conflict? One way to structure that conversation is to ask each source the exploratory questions that were posed during the initial theological interrogation of the topic.

Taking a Stand

6. By this point in a seminar most participants have some opinion about the discussion. These may have been noted earlier, but this is a time to focus on the question "What do you believe about . . . ?"

The expression of beliefs or opinions may uncover differences and lead to cognitive as well as emotional dissonance. The dissonance is the gap in which discoveries are made. Sometimes they ooze out like hot lava, and sometimes they erupt with fanfare and emotion. It is important, however, that beliefs be heard without passing judgment. Judging one another's beliefs inhibits the free-flow information. It is a time to listen and be considerate. The mere act of respectful listening does not have to indicate support for or agreement with a particular statement. Respectful listening does provide an arena in which ideas may be safely expressed, examined, and perhaps even modified.

Conclusion

7. What has been learned? What is new information? How have perspectives been influenced? Have there been any moments when

something caused someone to say "Wow!" This is a time to reap the insights of the conversation.

Consequences

8. Consequences have a twofold outcome. The first consequence is (a) the decision of the individual who has reached an insight and is making a decision. The second consequence is (b) the effect of that decision on others.

a) Learning something new may be pleasant or at least gratifying. Now comes an opportunity to examine the consequences. This comes in two parts. The first part involves the personal results, implications, or decisions of those who are part of the discussion. What are they to do with the information or insights that have been acquired?

b) The second part of examining consequences is to consider how they may affect others. If a course of action is to be pursued, who is needed to provide support? What will be the impact on those around us—family, friends, and colleagues? What impact might this make on the larger world? For instance, if someone decides that a call to mission work is indicated, whom will this affect? How might that mission work affect those who will be the beneficiaries of this ministry?

Closure

9. Celebrate the moment and make commitments.
10. Give thanks and depart.

This general outline can be initiated at any of the four major source points, as noted in the specific methods detailed in the Appendices.

TECHNIQUES

Knowing the outline, however, is not sufficient to lead theological reflection for a seminar. This section describes various elements of the outline and the techniques that will help a group develop its own methods for learning how to think theologically.

Personal and Internal

What is personal and internally construed in our lives is generally hidden until we select to reveal it either consciously or subconsciously. Overtly what are at stake in theological reflection, however, are the conscious and intentional offerings someone is willing to make to the process. The technique by which this is attained is that of telling our stories. For some this can be very difficult because the accounts that offer learning opportunities are the personal stories of the individuals in the group. A reflection group needs to be careful that it is not relying on other people's experiences. Telling about events in other people's lives may be showing an interest, but usually it is closer to gossip. Neither interest in the lives of others nor gossip is appropriate material for theological reflection.

BEGINNING FROM AN ACTION

When we begin a reflection from something we have done or experienced, we must find a way of relating that event to others in the seminar. Doing this is to engage in the art of storytelling. It is a skill, like that of writing effective accounts. In this case we are talking about biographical stories, of course. The storyteller needs to say what happened. It is not very helpful to editorialize or to muse over how it happened. To provide justification by pointing to the causes dilutes the power of the narrative. When a story is well told, the why and how will become apparent or will not be essential to the story. It may be helpful to ask the storyteller questions such as: What happened? Who was there? What did you do? When did it occur? What did you see? What was the sequence of events? What was the response? What did you hear? What did you smell? What did you feel? What did you think? Of course, no narration truly depicts an event. The same event told by the same narrator will seem different to different listeners, regardless of whether they hear the account together or at different venues. The reason is that the narration itself is an unrepeatable event, and each listener may hear something slightly different, because each person in the audience brings a different perspective.

FINDING AN EVENT TO NARRATE

Selecting a significant event is critical to relating a story that originated in a personal experience. Often significant events that do not qualify as major life crises offer an excellent occasion for profound learning. Stories about occurrences that relate major events such as a sudden loss of job, the announcement of a major illness, or even something pleasant like a marriage announcement are usually not very good places from which to initiate a reflection. Should someone bring that kind of event to a seminar for theological reflection, it may be best to listen to the account, relate to it, and perhaps pray with the person. But we should refrain from a theological inquiry until the event has receded. The high level of emotion associated with such an event will block much creative reflection, because it is still lively.

It is very difficult to reflect effectively when in the midst of the experience. One has to step back to reflect. Events that are still in process are not good opportunities for theological reflection. They may easily degenerate into looking at the problem that is posed by the circumstances and then seeking to engage in problem-solving. While solving problems is a worthy endeavor, that is not theological reflection.

OFFERING A PERSONAL BELIEF FOR REFLECTION

Our beliefs are precious, particularly if they are deeply felt. To alter what we believe may produce life-changing decisions. Consequently, the most difficult place to begin a theological reflection is with our personal beliefs. We are accustomed to stating what we believe if we feel safe and even to debating those beliefs. But we are not accustomed to permitting someone to examine those beliefs with us and then to hold them up to a theological analysis. Consequently, beginning a reflection from someone's personal and deeply cherished beliefs should be undertaken only if great trust exists in the group.

When someone offers a personal belief for a reflection, it must not be argued or debated. It is there to be examined for the purpose of learning. That is best done through the experiences we have encountered that relate us to that belief. What we can do is examine the belief with theological questions, such as those proposed in the chapter concerning this.

Communal/External: Beginning a Reflection from External Sources

The external sources for reflection come from the world we inhabit. As we have already noted, we distinguish between the external sources associated with our Christian tradition and those associated with the rest of the world. We also recognize that these are not always so neatly separated. Cultures outside Christianity have affected our faith, and Christianity has affected the secular world.

BEGINNING WITH TRADITION

The tradition is a favorite source for those who prefer to deal with what their historical faith proclaims before examining their own lives. It is also a good place to initiate a reflection if participants had anticipated that the reflection process would be a Bible study rather than a theological exploration.

Beginning with tradition does pose a series of questions, such as:

Whose tradition? The traditions of the Christian faith are not the same for everyone. Some root all their faith in the Bible. But even the Bible is not uniform among all Christian groups. Some recognize the Old Testament Apocrypha as a significant aspect of the biblical tradition; others tend to ignore the apocryphal texts. Usually those who include them in the tradition also include significant historical texts, such as the creeds of the Church and liturgical materials. Still others include selections from the entire experience of the history of Christianity, because it all represents God's interaction with the communion of saints that form the Church.

How to access the tradition? If the tradition is limited to biblical texts, access is fairly easy, since the Bible is a very accessible text. But even here consideration of the different translations and versions of the Bible is important. One aspect of a reflection is to examine different renditions of a text. That may be done between translations or, if the expertise is present, between language traditions, such as the Greek text, the Latin text, and the English text. In addition, it may be possible to compare texts within the Bible itself, since there is duplication, with differences, of many biblical passages, for example, the parables, the events of Christmas, and the experience of Good Friday/Easter.

Accessing materials that are not biblical may be more difficult. Various collections—some in one volume, others that fill library shelves—are available. Documents from Church history are also available on the Internet.

When using a text for reflection, it is vital to select a passage that is sufficiently narrow and accessible to all in the seminar. To try to focus on an entire book in the Bible or even on a chapter may be more than can be undertaken in a single session. As a careful series of reflections proceeds, however, the larger interpretation can develop.

Beginning a Reflection from a Communal Resource

Culture: Culture is such a variable that it is useful to narrow the aspect of culture to be examined at any given time. Perhaps it will come from politics or from journalism. It may come from the arts or from advertising. Again, it is vital to narrow the field and pinpoint the object of reflection. It may be useful to focus on a single item, such as an advertisement or a particular event. Once again, it is vital that everyone in the seminar has access to the same information. If someone tells about the cultural item, then the common experience of the narration, not the cultural item itself, becomes the focus.

The problems: Earlier I introduced the problem caused by the fact that we inhabit a universe bombarded by a plethora of cultures. While we may differentiate between cultures, some ours and some not, I think it is safe to consider a culture of which we have knowledge to have somehow integrated into our own and to have affected us in some way. Therefore I suggest that it is not helpful to consider any cultural text to be exterior to ourselves. Of course, our degree of involvement may be radically different. For example, almost everyone knows today of the Japanese fondness for raw fish known as sushi. This is a cultural aspect of Japan that has quickly integrated into Western culture. It does not mean that everyone wants to eat sushi, but it does affect us even if our reaction is one of "Ugh! I wouldn't eat raw fish."

THE CONFUSION

It is not always easy to differentiate between culture and tradition. In general, Christianity has tended over time to integrate significant cultural norms with a kind of baptismal acceptance. For instance, in the United States the cultural holiday of Thanksgiving has been thoroughly integrated into religious rituals. In other places that kind of integration was achieved by celebrating the days of saints or with agricultural celebrations named after saints, such as that of St. Michael's, which comes after the harvest in northern Europe is completed.

NATURE

The natural resources—even something as common as a leaf, a flower, or a rock—may serve as a source to initiate a theological reflection. While nature may not be part of culture, it is part of the world we experience and often serves metaphorically for various aspects of our lives. Food substances from nature have long served in this way. Bread, wine, or the raw materials of wheat and grapes frequently appear in religious texts as part of that text's reflection. Such items became means to express the deeper meaning of the relationship to God and the divine milieu.

WHAT THEOLOGICAL REFLECTION IS NOT

This is a refrain, but it is vital to remember that a theological reflection is not a debate, with points to be scored. It is not a solution to a problem. It is not a course of therapy, and it is not an academic exercise. Theological reflection is a meaningful conversation that leads to insights about the present and opens possibilities for the future within a context of Christian theology. When done well through a disciplined reflection, our theology comes alive in the context of the experiences of our lives. Both the dramatic and the mundane are seen in a new way. We develop a way of taking all life more seriously while enjoying and appreciating it more.

METAPHORICAL LANGUAGE

Few things give students more difficulty when doing theological reflection than grappling with the notion of developing their own metaphors. Yet once students acquire this skill, their ability to explore theology at all levels is greatly enhanced. I like to think of theology as rationalized art form. Unlike law and philosophy, where reason dominates, theology dwells at once in the heart and the mind. Theology that is purely rational is sterile, and a faith that is purely emotive is puerile. Both can be demonic.

One way to overcome the mind-heart/reason-faith dichotomy is through language that transcends. The bridges that provide transcendence are made of metaphors and images. These become the stories and foundational myths of our civilization. That is why ultimately language is metaphorical at its root. Language seeks to express what we experience, and at the heart of the experience is what we do, what we feel, and what we think, something we express to others through communications that are at once verbal and symbolic. Metaphors that express our deepest ideas in the form of symbols and stories literally "carry us across" and provide transcendence (the root meaning of *metaphor* is "to carry with or across").

The transcendent conjunctions that provide the metaphorical bridges are not easy to create, however. The words we use often refer to something beyond the language, and they may carry multiple meanings. Words should not be confused with the reality to which they refer, which is a frequent mistake of those who interpret language in a literal fashion. Words are symbolic expressions by which we denote the reference. Language thus acts as a bridge, so that people can communicate by using sounds, signs, and symbols. But with theology we seek to cross a wider chasm. We bridge from the world of the people of God to the realm of the kingdom of God. Our bridge is through image, through metaphors, and through symbols wrapped into stories that form the basis of mythology, those stories to which life is true, even if they are not true to life.

Ultimately theology works with and through metaphors. For a highly reasoned, educated people, this can be most difficult when they expect concrete answers to their questions and aspirations. It can also be threatening, because when we reach into our creativity, we may reveal and discover aspects of ourselves we would prefer to avoid. We may even discover aspects of ourselves we did not know existed, because our powers to reason often mask our deepest creative and destructive urges. Such creative occasions may produce awe and wonder. They are the fountainheads of creativity, but whenever we have an "Aha" experience, we also recognize that we are no longer fully in control of the process. To feel that sense of loss of control that artists feel when expressing creativity is at once illuminating, frightening, and energizing. The experience raises our adrenaline level; it excites, and it invigorates.

THE USE OF METAPHORS

Regardless of where we begin—with action, with a text, with culture, or with belief—it is very difficult to reflect directly on our experience. Until our reflection actually touches us where we live, it is merely "academic." To achieve a reflection requires that we construct a mirror image. Metaphors are the building blocks for bridges that can relate us to the transcendent, first to others and so ultimately to the divine. Thus metaphors can represent the truth about something we have experienced in a manner that can truly change our perspective, because we are able to perceive our experience in a broader way.

The use of metaphors, of course, is basic to all communications. Our languages are symbolic and ultimately either imitative or metaphorical. When language imitates a sound, it is a direct representation. But most language is based upon the development of sophisticated symbols. The images we create linguistically can even convey a sense of odor, taste, color, ambience, mood, or emotion. To move beyond the daily data of life we use symbolic language, language that carries us across our own thresholds. That symbolic image links us to one another by recognizing the commonality of our different experiences, and so imparts a sense of belonging to a created order. We each have our place, but we are also linked to one another by our languages, verbal as well as nonverbal. For Christians the ultimate linkage is that divine connection that forms us to become the people of God. Metaphors thus can become the first step, for they help us to make a bridge from the world of our mundane experience to the kingdom of God.

ISSUES

For some, images or metaphors serve as the best vehicle to make theological connections; for others, another kind of abstraction works better. Issues that are stated as bifocal propositions containing the tensions of our existence can serve as metaphors. This is a technical use of the word "issue," quite different from the general understanding of an issue as a matter to be debated or resolved, as for example the issue of capital punishment.

In the context of theological reflection, an issue is a balanced statement that reveals how we are caught in conflicting demands. Just as a metaphor can picture our human condition, so an issue statement can express our predicaments. Paul expressed it clearly when he spoke about our failure to achieve the good we wish to accomplish and our propensity to do wrong even when we try our best. A personal example of an issue for me is that I travel to accomplish my work. That brings me great joy and fruitful outcomes, but I also enjoy being at home. Here is an issue, then, that may express what this is about. I enjoy doing my job, and I love to be with my family. Other examples of issues are:

- I want discipline in my life, and I want to be free and creative in my expression.
- I want to be myself, but I want to behave in an acceptable manner.
- I want to enjoy a life of leisure, but I want to be gainfully employed.

All these are issues that express tensions under which we live. They are universal, but they also have particular applications that can be defined and identified in my life.

WORKING WITH ISSUES

When an issue statement is created, we can use it to proceed with our reflection process in at least two very different ways. The first is to ask theological questions, such as are suggested in the next chapter. So, for example, one might pose the question: "In this issue, what does the world look like?" (creation); or "In this issue, what do we find to be destructive?" (sin).

Issue statements, however, are very useful tools to examine the implications of an event from the point of view of moral theology. To do this, the dimensions of the issue need to be explored. Each of the two major clauses of an issue statement must be examined separately. Usually it is helpful to chart this by establishing two columns under each clause, one labeled "Cost" and the other "Promise." There are thus four columns to be considered. When this is done, often the information that evolves will help discern the moral implications of an action. In another context it may be helpful to label the columns under each clause with the words "Risk" and "Opportunity."

The issue statements described above are bifocal or two-valued expressions. When an issue describes a situation, it does so in terms of either/or or both/and, thereby restricting the descriptions to only two aspects. In actuality, life is much more complex. I may enjoy my work and I may enjoy being at home. But I also appreciate many other opportunities, such as playing sports, attending a musical performance, or visiting with friends. If the issue describes the tension of accepting a new position or staying in the present one, there are other possibilities that may be part of the situation, such as looking for other opportunities, retirement, or simply not working. The feasibility (cost and promise or risk and opportunity) of each of these will quickly eliminate some options. I may be too young to retire, or other work opportunities may not be available. But the fact remains: there are many ways to say yes to the decisions we face.

CONCLUDING A THEOLOGICAL REFLECTION

Finally, a word needs to be added about conclusions. So many conversations, theological and otherwise, are left dangling. That may be acceptable in the daily interchanges we all experience, but it becomes a frustration when consciously engaged in an educational venture.

If a theological reflection has progressed sufficiently so that metaphors are part of the discussion and participants have observed connections with theological texts or disciplines, then it may be possible to bring it to a fruitful and satisfying conclusion. Some simple questions can serve to bring closure. First it is important to briefly recapitulate where the conversation has arrived. Then these questions are useful:

> What have we learned?
> What insights have occurred to us as we proceeded thus far?
> What strikes a chord in this conversation?

If there is time, it may be possible to take those questions another step by inquiring about the importance of the insights that may be gleaned and how they may be put to use. The point of this final postscript, how-ever, is to emphasize that there is almost always something to learn and that it is important to take the time and effort to glean from those pre-cious opportunities to learn. When we fail to accomplish the harvest, we have lost all the efforts that produced the crop.

One way to reap the harvest of learning is through prayer, and this formula is a helpful technique. At the end of the reflection, just ask the group to contribute to each clause of the following prayer:

Informed by the reflection we have just completed
> God is . . .
> We pray for . . .
> In order that . . .
> Amen.

THE ROLE OF PLAY

Finally, I add one important caveat. Engaging in theological reflec-tion is a serious endeavor, but it is often better done when we are re-laxed. Often when we are playful with our seeking, we uncover new significance. The sign of laughter is an omen of relaxation to the kind of openness that makes it possible to explore new ground, new thoughts, and new patterns of life. It may not be possible to design how members of a seminar will react, but it is possible to engender an atmosphere that values play and encourages laughter.

CHAPTER 13

Asking Theological Questions

The Theological Interrogatory

The examination of life may be done from many points of view. But to make that examination theological, one must ask the questions that emerge from the discipline or science of theology. Those form what I call a "theological interrogatory." The basis for the interrogatory rests in the traditional topics of theological discourse, the great themes of our faith. These are addressed differently under different circumstances, even within Holy Scripture. First, theologians discriminate, for instance, between the doctrine of salvation in the Old Testament and the doctrine of salvation in the New Testament. Second, a functional theology develops as a kind of continual event. Theology is always in motion as it reflects our deepest interpretations of an ever changing universe and our place in it. The basic interrogatory, however, remains fairly constant. While new aspects may arise, most of it is defined within that body of tradition we normally refer to as systematic theology.

Theologians have usually developed a systematic theology, or at least certain aspects of it, and then presented that to the Church. That is to say, professional theologians have framed the questions and then provided the answers. But if there truly exists a *vox populi* and a *consensus fidelium,* then theology must operate from a wider spectrum. That becomes possible, even critical, today because we possess amazing electronic means to access the necessary information. By teaching how to pose the right questions, we can make use of that information. Teaching how to frame the questions is the equivalent of teaching someone to fish. The skill will last a lifetime. Since all faithful people are theologians, we must provide the tools for critical theological thinking. Knowing how to frame the proper questions in the most helpful manner is crucial to the task.

Theology as a Scientific Activity

Theology is an activity to be engaged rather than the acceptance of conclusions prepared and digested in advance. Everyone participates in theological reflection in some fashion, so we might as well learn something about doing it properly as a discipline rather than a necessary whim. Education in this area is distinctive and helpful in its own way, just as teaching physiology and medicine can help people to take precautions and remedy their maladies or recognize the need for professional assistance. This means that we no longer leave all the decisions to the professional interpreters but recognize that we have a role in interpreting our own salvation, just as we have a role in making decisions about our medical care. The primary role of the professional is to provide the proper tools. In this case, the tools are the outlines for the discipline and the questions that evoke discovery.

The Doctrine of Creation

QUESTIONS ABOUT THE UNIVERSE: OUR RELATIONSHIP TO THE WORLD

Theological questions about the universe are fairly simple to pose but difficult to answer. Ultimately they are cosmological, and that is a grand and complex stage. To ask theological questions with an expectation that we will receive definitive and final answers produces only complete nonsense. For example, to ask the question "What kind of a God permits suffering?" is to pose a question that is hypothetical and too grandiose to answer definitively, even though everyone knows that suffering is part of our existence. But to understand what kind of a world it is that contains the suffering that has happened in a particular set of events, such as an earthquake or a flood, or in some other event, such as war, focuses the question to a more manageable level. The key, then, is to focus the question clearly on a particular event in order to derive a useful response. This brings us to look at the possibilities for some major questions around traditional theological topics.

The doctrine of Creation traditionally provides responses that describe the world we inhabit and experience. The basis for it begins in the very first words of the Book of Genesis. Some questions about the doctrine of Creation are:

- What kind of world does this event describe?
- As we look at an event, where is there good and evil in this world?
- What are the expectations?

Example: Nature produces tragedies. The Creation is both destructive and creative.

THE FAILURE OF NATURE, THEODICY

Nothing is more difficult than to explain the suffering of the innocent. When an earthquake occurs and buildings collapse, we seek to blame the architects, engineers, and builders. When the weather produces great storms, we blame the meteorologist for not giving sufficient warning. In other words, we try to find someone to blame so that the suffering will have an explanation.

No matter how vigilant we may be, natural forces will still produce suffering, destruction, and death. We may avert death, but when statisticians say that death was averted because new medical advances are available or because a safety problem was eliminated, they are always wrong. Death was only delayed. Changes, of which birth and death are the major ones, are always occurring. Many of these changes are part of the natural order. Thus we may be driven to ask, "Why would a loving God allow things like a tornado to occur?"

How we view Creation and the problem of theodicy tends to color all subsequent decisions. We may view God's handiwork as good and benevolent. In that case we are disappointed and bitter when a destructive moment arises. We may view nature as evil, something to tame and dominate for the good of humanity. In that case natural evil does not surprise us, but we may become very frustrated because we are fighting ourselves. We are part of nature. There are no unnatural substances, and we cannot separate ourselves from our environment.

Still another way is to view nature as God's gift and thus beyond our total understanding. We may master certain aspects, but much will remain untamed and uncontrolled. Our task is to live within the bounds of these limitations. That then brings us to the next topic, the doctrine of humanity. Nature is good and bountiful and we are strangers in a strange land, sojourners and recipients of a gift. Evil in that case becomes anything that tends to destroy the purity of the gift.

The Doctrine of Humanity

QUESTIONS ABOUT HUMANITY (THE DOCTRINE OF HUMANITY)

Human activity can be interpreted. We develop our interpretations on the basis of our experience. Thus the words rooted in one experience may convey something the speaker did not intend to someone who is listening with a point of view based on a very different set of experiences. Consequently, theological terminology concerned with the doctrine of humanity needs careful explication. Words that apply to the doctrine of humanity, like sin, judgment, repentance, and redemption, require definitions that may differ from commonly accepted parlance. In general, those words are loaded with meaning; consequently they tend to convey multiple messages, especially in a theological context. In theological discourses it is essential to establish how the terms are used. The emotional impact those words carry may blur our understanding of them unless we are precise in our usage.

As a starting point, the human condition may be described as being in SIN (*sin* uppercase), and it generally describes what is meant by original sin. This expression is easily misunderstood because it is frequently confused with sexuality, and we must be careful to avoid it. We did not inherit original sin, but we were born with it. It is not an alibi for moral failure but a statement about our human situation, about our limitations. Recognizing our original sin is the same as accepting that we are not divine. Our human limitations lead us to failures that cause ourselves and others pain and sorrow.

Questions that lead to examining the human condition may be:

- What in this event describes the human dilemma that cannot be avoided?
- What are the built-in conditions of this situation?

HUMAN FAILURE (SIN)

Human failure (*sin* lowercase) is more difficult to describe than that simple three-lettered word "sin" suggests. Often we think that sin equals moral failure or ethical wrongdoing and breaking human or divine law. Often, indeed usually, these are sins, but sin encompasses much more. Sin is also those failures that we did not intend, those moments of distress we imposed on others and yet were unaware, and those destructive acts that are unavoidable because the alternative would be even more destructive (e.g., choosing the lesser of two evils or the best of two goods). This may paint a bleak picture, but the fact is that we are not able to control the universe precisely because we are human and not divine. The result is that we participate in destructive activities, and regardless of motives or awareness, these are sins.

Questions that may evoke our understanding of sin are those involving terms like:

- What is destructive?
- What causes pain?
- Where do we find alienation and discord?

GOD'S ACTION: JUDGMENT

"Judgment" is a term that thoroughly confuses most people because it is often considered to be punishment. In a theological context, judgment is what brings us to awareness that something is wrong. Punishment may be assigned to provide notice and emphasis about wrongdoing, but punishment may have other qualities. Reparation, retribution, vengeance, and repayment of debt are also aspects of punishment. The phrase "The felon has paid his duty to society" suggests that the judgment is primarily punishment, repayment, and ransom. In the context of theology, however, judgment first serves as a learning experience that leads to a sense of guilt and a willingness to atone and change.

Judgment comes to us all the time. Usually it is minor and goes unnoticed. But any time we are made to "stop, look, and listen" we have an opportunity to make decisions. As a result, we select to act in one way or another, and that is the consequence of judgment having been visited on us. In this context, judgment may come with a friendly word, a natural catastrophe, a rebuke, an examination, an illness, or an act of charity. What makes it judgment is that we have had to think about our activity and reconsider those things we are doing that are destructive.

Some of the questions that elicit judgment are:

- What calls me up short?
- What makes me notice that something is happening?
- What is the large plank that struck me between the eye as if I were a mule not paying attention?
- What in my life gets my attention as if it were a railroad semaphore blinking and clanking to announce that a train is coming down the track toward my intersection?

REPENTANCE[1]

Repentance is the human response to divine action through judgment. God speaks through those events that bring judgment, and

1. The English language uses the letters *re* to denote the repetition of an action. This causes some difficulties in theology with words such as "resurrection"

human beings have an opportunity to respond. Some questions that lead to consideration of this are:

- What response can be made?
- Where or to whom should forgiveness be extended?
- What actions should be taken to make things just and right?

REDEMPTION/SALVATION/CELEBRATION

Redemption has been cheapened in English by such terms as "redemption coupons," so that it often carries a sense of buying back or exchange. This has been confused in theology by some doctrines that suggest that Jesus Christ purchased human salvation through his self-offering on the cross and thereby satisfied a debt on behalf of all human beings.

Redemption has a sense of freeing or loosening someone from bondage, not unlike the dismissal of a case in court. Salvation is the post-dismissal opportunity for new life, and that is an occasion for celebration. That brings us to look at events with a new set of theological questions, questions about freedom, opportunity, and celebration. Some examples are:

- What frees us?
- What offers new life and opportunity?
- What is an occasion for giving thanks?
- What is the moment to enjoy the gifts we have received?
- What is there to celebrate and be joyful about?

Questions About the Nature of God

The high point of theological doctrines has always come around the questions: What can we say about God, or who is God? Theologians

---

and "repentance." The Greek terms behind the English translations convey something slightly, but significantly, different. "Resurrection" translates the Greek word *anastasis*, which is better translated by English phrases such as "raising up" or "raising anew." "Repentance" translates the Greek word metanoia, which is better translated as "a change of mind or perspective, a turning around." "Redemption" translates the Greek *lusis*, which translates better as "loosening" or another English word with *re*, "release." Thus it implies a letting go, dismissal, or freeing, which the English does not convey so effectively. What I want to emphasize is that, while the English words tend to suggest a replication of the past, the theological understanding of the words as they emerge from the more ancient Greek uses is that the past does not return. The future is always new and therefore full of hope.

have sought to respond to these questions in a variety of ways, not the least of which are the celebrated arguments for the existence of God formulated by theologians like Anselm of Canterbury and Thomas Aquinas during the Middle Ages. Much later philosophers like Immanuel Kant and Georg F. Hegel, among others, sought to derive arguments for the existence of God by using philosophical arguments. Our point in terms of theological reflection, however, is not so much to develop arguments for the existence of God as to point to occasions when we can legitimately interpret events and say that God's activity has been experienced.

The Christian doctrine of God divides into three components, normally thought of as the Trinity. There exists a distinction between the three components, but they are also framed and held together within a certain unity that characterizes the Trinity. While other religions do not use the figures of Father, Son, and Holy Spirit, one can find aspects of them in most doctrines of salvation. Because two of those terms are male, today we can see that this relationship of distinctiveness and unity that characterizes the Christian understanding of God can be expressed in other terms, terms that suggest that God is not always best expressed by masculine terminology.

THE DOCTRINE OF GOD AS CREATOR

The creative functions are best examined through the following questions:

- What is productive?
- What invites growth and new life?
- What is innovative and exciting?
- Where do we find the love that puts things in motion?

THE DOCTRINE OF CHRIST

Questions about the doctrine of Christ invite an opportunity to encounter Christ in life's events. Some examples are:

- Where have you seen Jesus Christ?
- What reminds you of Christ?
- Where and when are you invited to reach for whole(holy)ness?
- Where do we find the love that makes new what is broken?

THE DOCTRINE OF THE HOLY SPIRIT

The gifts of the Spirit are listed by Paul in 1 Corinthians 13. These can lead to a series of useful questions. Among them are:

- What and where is wisdom?
- Where is there knowledge spoken truthfully?
- Where is there faith, the courage to proceed amidst uncertainty?
- Where is there healing?
- What speaks truth forth in a clear manner, like a prophet?
- What or who tends to bring clarity to the diversity and apparent tumult?
- Where do we find the love that binds us together?

GRACE

Finally we may also ask questions about grace in all its fullness. To raise questions about grace is to raise questions about what is graceful or full of grace. Some sample questions are:

- For what should we give thanks?
- What gives rise to being gracious or grateful (the two words are cognates)?
- Where is our own opportunity to offer ourselves (our souls and bodies) as an expression of our gratefulness?

Using the Theological Interrogatory

Asking theological questions such as I have proposed above invites us to examine what happens to us through the lenses of theology. Sometimes those questions can be posed in very mundane terms, but they become theologically significant when we recognize that they link back to standard theological assertions, most of them very ancient.

What makes our endeavor theological as a science as well as faithful, that is to say, a formal study of theology and also a loyal response to our vows, is that we look at life's events through a doctrinal lens. Posing questions is the way we use those lenses to examine what is happening, what we do, how we relate to others, how we live, and what our relationship to God happens to be at any given moment. No single occasion for theological reflection can use all the questions, just as no single medical examination can look at all aspects of human physiology. Selectivity is necessary. When we find an important track, we can pursue it and explore. Our goal is to develop our own theological matrix, which we can use to assess life's twists and turns, disappointments and moments of joy, and those deepest and most profound moments of birth, death, and new life.

The application of theological questions may be made at each point of the four-source model. That is to say, we may ask these questions of the metaphor that was evoked from the narration of an event in our lives. We may ask these questions of our beliefs (i.e., given a particular belief, what kind of a world is it in which we hold that belief?). We may also ask these questions about specific elements of our Christian tradition or of cultural perspectives. In this manner the theological interrogatory becomes the lens that bring into perspective all our life's experiences. That makes it a distinctive set of lenses because they cross all other disciplines. Where growth and learning take place, however, is not in the focus on an individual point from any of the sources but in the fertile dialogue that takes place as we compare and contrast the various conclusions. When we find congruence and dissonance, we discover opportunities for affirming what we know, and we uncover possibilities for something new.

CHAPTER 14

Guiding Theological Reflections

The Skills of a Mentor

Posing the right question in a helpful manner and at the appropriate moment is a fundamental educational skill that is fundamental to guiding a seminar through a reflective process or to teaching others how to guide seminars. But guiding a reflection requires more than technical skills. Theological reflection requires organization, leadership, and interpersonal skills. The guide or mentor may both teach the methods and guide the process, but ultimately learning how to lead theological reflection and leading a seminar using a process of reflection are two separate things. Both, however, are extensions of the educational process of learning how to engage in theological reflection. They are best learned as part of an action/reflection model of education, a model that begins the learning process by engaging in an activity that is then critiqued. That critique, however, is as much about personal style and effectiveness as it is about the activity itself. All the components of effective communications are at play—content, tonality, language, emotions, context, and even the body language of posture and gestures.

The First Mentor

In these pages the word "mentor" is often used to describe the leader of a theological reflection, because it best describes the function of a guide or leader of a seminar. The word "mentor" has an interesting origin as a proper name. Mentor was a friend of Odysseus, who lived on the Greek island of Ithaca. When he left his home and wife to go on his long voyage, Odysseus left Mentor in charge of the household, with the special responsibility of raising his son, Telemachus. The story takes an interesting twist, for the legend relate that Athena, the Greek goddess of wisdom, taught Telemachus through the person of Mentor. In other words, Mentor was serving as a conduit for divine wisdom. He taught more with questions than with information, and he acted more like a guide or tutor than like a lecturer. That explains why someone leading a theological reflection may best be known by the terminology of "mentor" or perhaps "tutor," someone who shows the way. A mentor conveys information and also empowers the student to take charge of that knowledge.

The Qualities of a Mentor

What I have already said about the origin of the term "mentor" suggests some of the qualities a mentor needs to possess. Some of what follows should be obvious. The mentor of a group needs to be familiar with the subject matter under scrutiny. A mentor also needs to be at ease with the methods required to pursue a reflection from the beginning to a successful conclusion, identifying what has been learned and what might be done with that information. Finally, a mentor needs to know how to interact with people so that a trusting climate for learning is established for the group. That requires knowledge of how groups function, comfort with the fact that conflict is part of group life, and patience to suffer the difficult times that are an inevitable part of the learning process.

The Personal Attributes of a Mentor

A mentor, like any teacher, must possess certain personal attributes to be successful. Much of this is no more and no less than personal maturity, self-understanding, and stability, combined with personal discipline and a sense of humor. In other words, an effective mentor knows how to be comfortable with other people and yet is not self-centered or dominant.

Vulnerability

Perhaps no characteristic is more important to be an effective mentor than being vulnerable. When we make ourselves available, open to others, and share our own personal and difficult moments, we become vulnerable. There are those aspects of our lives that are known and of which we are aware; this is where we are open and creative with others. There are other aspects of our lives, however, that we need to reveal if we are to enlarge the possibilities for creative interaction. Vulnerability is the willingness to open those secret aspects of life as it becomes appropriate to do when we are engaged in an exchange with others.[1] When we are open, we make it possible for others to do the same.

To be vulnerable, mentors must be intellectually aware and emotionally involved, which means that they must be self-aware, especially of their personal emotions. Vulnerability alone, however, does not suffice. Mentors must also understand the dynamics of group process.

A mentor who cannot accept conflict or understand a challenge to his or her authority as part of the process will become too controlling or just give up. A mentor who must "fix" everything will not succeed, because the group will not be able to take responsibility for its life and its opportunities to learn. On the other hand, a mentor who is detached will evoke that same detachment from others, and the life of the seminar will flag for lack of commitment.

Openness to Other Ideas

Most people think it is valuable to be open to other ideas; however, when those ideas counter our own most cherished beliefs, it becomes difficult to empathize. We like to think that our beliefs are correct or "right." Mentors need the skills to listen and separate their ideas from those expressed by others. They also need to possess the self-confidence that permits them not to respond, to negate, deny, or rebut what others express. The risk, of course, is that a failure to respond may be interpreted as an agreement when that is not the case, so there comes a time when it becomes important to express differences. But a mentor, in the course of leading others in reflection, often needs to withhold from expressing judgments on the offerings of others too quickly.

Knowledge of the Subject Matter

A mentor leads reflections about a particular topic or body of knowledge. To do this, a mentor needs to possess a familiarity and comfort with the subject matter of the discipline, but a mentor does not need to be

---

1. Becoming appropriately vulnerable is not to ask for confession, although it has confessional overtones. The word "appropriate" is the key qualifier. It is not appropriate to reveal others' painful secrets while sharing one's own life. It is also important to gauge what is appropriate to reveal about one's personal life. Too much revelation too easily given becomes exhibitionism. Usually, however, we err on the side of caution in such matters. There exists a tension between revealing information that will strain or block a relationship and the reality that we can be freer with one another and more creative when secrecy is minimized.

an expert on all its phases or specialties to help others learn. Everyone in a seminar brings expertise and is part of the teaching/learning process. The best mentor will lead participants in a seminar to discover the contents through their involvement with the course of study. The leader or mentor has the role of providing a safe terrain for the inevitable encounters when differences arise by helping the group discover common ground on which to work and learn.

Reflection Skills

Any mentor needs to possess a number of skills to be effective. These divide into two categories: group dynamics and methods of reflection. The most basic is an understanding of how groups work and what some of the dynamics of any group can bring. Understanding the dynamics of a group is a useful skill that applies to any venture that involves other people. It is best taught by providing experiences that are followed by a disciplined reflection. Often a momentary experience can be the grist for an extended reflection and productive results. What follows are some of the most basic aspects of these dynamics.

Group Dynamics

GROUP LIFE

A typical group gathers in response to an invitation. Some typical questions arise immediately:

- What is this about?
- What will it cost?
- Where are the bathrooms?
- How does someone call me in case of an emergency?
- When will this end?

Behind these questions is another set of questions that are usually internalized but not articulated until later:

- Do I belong here?
- Who is in charge?
- What is expected of me?
- What will I gain?
- Is this a safe place?
- Will others like me?

- What will I get out of this?
- Will my personal needs be met?
- What will happen if I challenge the program?

These questions usually arise in a different form after the group has begun to work. Some typical questions at this next stage of group life might be:

- What is your experience as a leader?
- Can we have regular breaks?
- Who assigned this textbook anyway?
- What happens if I can't come or I come late?

This is a normal pattern, because groups have lives that develop just as people develop. There is infancy, individuation, maturation, productivity, aging, and returning to dependency. The questions above are some of the questions that arise with dependency, which is always the first stage of a group's life. Of course, many groups do not pass through all phases of group life, but effective reflection groups must attain some level of stable and mature productivity to be successful.

It is very helpful to realize that groups begin life as infants, dependent upon the person perceived to be in charge. That dependency, however, usually leads to conflict with the leader or perceived leader, or even with a safe surrogate. When that counter-dependency rises to the surface, the life of the group is beginning to develop. Like dealing with an unruly teenager who is seeking to find an identity, the counter-dependency phase in a group's life can be uncomfortable or even frightening for the leadership as well as for members of the group. Those who react with fear tend to respond in one of two ways. They may fall into the trap of exercising or demanding strong controls, or they may try to escape the conflict. The fear produces what is classically known as the fight/flight dilemma. Neither is especially productive. In a seminar the mentor should remain firm and keep the discussion venue safe. That requires setting a tone of care and support that allows the group to develop the conflict and work through it. In some cases the conflict will first emerge in passive behaviors such as arriving late, going to sleep, or finding excuses to diminish participation. But passive behavior can mask the underlying anger.

When the conflict becomes overt, it may first aim at safe targets, preferably someone or something not present. It may come in the form of attacks on the materials in use, blaming an author who is not present, or it may come with questions about the processes or even the personality of individuals, especially the perceived leader. When a group works through these moments of conflict, there frequently develops a period of euphoria that is unrealistic, although it can be very energizing and the occasion for a lot of good humor. Many church conferences end after this euphoric moment has been reached. But at this point the group is at a sophomoric stage, a bit wise and also a bit foolish in its euphoria. They have discovered the joy of teamwork but have yet to deal with the requirements of a deep commitment.

As a group continues, a plateau may be attained as it begins to grapple with deeper issues. At this point major conflict may erupt. The mentor's role is to continue to keep the venue safe for learning and also to help the group identify basic common interests and agreements, sometimes by pushing the question and searching for what various participants hold as ultimate values. When a group can engage its differences and work effectively, it has reached maturation. It is at its highest productivity.

As groups look toward senescence and coming to an end, frequently the steps reverse. First the group returns to conflict over matters of authority and then eventually returns to a kind of dependency that we can identify with those moments of helplessness when we face death. The mentor's role at this juncture is assist the grieving process, to help say goodbye, and to commemorate and celebrate the community and what has been gained.

GROUP NEEDS

Groups have a life pattern, and they also have certain needs to persist and function. Those fall in three general areas: a task to accomplish, the relationships of group members, and the personal needs of individual participants. When these are not attended to, the group will cease to exist. Often in voluntary seminars there is a slow seepage of people who find "reasons" to curtail participation. Some early warning signs may be lateness, lack of participation, or unexplained absences, which become more frequent as time passes. A mentor can bring group needs to the attention of the community. These are community responsibilities. The mentor has the primary task of ensuring that they are on the table so that they will not be avoided or evaded.

Generally groups gather around something participants wish to accomplish. Clarity about this is important. The task needs to be perceived as worthwhile, and a plan to achieve it is necessary. In other words, an effective group possesses consensus and clarity about its purpose, knows how it will proceed and when it has completed its work.

Many groups, however, become task-oriented and fall into chaos because the relationships of the group's members become unpleasant. From time to time or at moments of crisis, it is important to examine and give attention to the interpersonal relationships in the group. How we share leadership, how we listen to one another, how we support one another, and how we celebrate our life together are all important aspects of maintaining group life. These must be addressed specifically, however, not as academic questions. It can be a very difficult and unpleasant process, but the fruits of working through interpersonal issues so that a team may form can galvanize a small community into a potent force.

Finally, no group can survive long without meeting personal needs. Some are obvious, like attending to physiological needs to take breaks, to nourish our bodies, and to obtain sufficient physical comfort. But that is not sufficient. Participants also need acceptance and affirmation. Moreover, they need to be participants and have some power and freedom so that they can provide effective contributions.

BELONGING

There are three aspects of personal needs: the need to belong, the need to have some control over what happens, and the need for affection. We can forgo some of these needs for a period of time, but if we feel that we are outcasts or that we are at someone else's mercy or that no one likes us, the desire is to flee to more pleasant circumstances. These three needs, of course, encompass two other needs that we all cherish: we want to be recognized and liked by others, and we want to maintain our freedom.

HOW TO DEVELOP A COMMUNITY OF LEARNING

So far we have presented elements of a seminar group or community of learning. What we should do to start is an important technique. It is not sufficient to say, "Here we are. Let's get started," and then expect things to develop. The ancient practice of telling stories around the campfire is something that we can adapt and use. First, however, a consensus about the purpose of the seminar and the process that is to be pursued needs to develop. One technique is to ask participants to articulate their expectations in writing. At a later date these expectations will serve as a checklist by which to evaluate what has happened in the life of the seminar. The check-in at a later date emphasizes that working out a seminar's expectations is not a one-time event. It is important for the learning community in a seminar to check with one another so that matters that affect the community may be attended.

Ultimately, however, the community needs that most important commodity—*trust*. We trust one another when we can be vulnerable in the presence of one another. One way to achieve trust is to reveal or tell our stories, our biographies. To be sure, what we share should be appropriate both in content and in form. The community will grow in trust and creativity as various members tell their stories. When we can express our thoughts and feelings, the isolation we initially feel dissipates, for we discover our common heritages, our common pains, our common joys, and our common desires.

HOW TO END A COMMUNITY OF LEARNING

Death is difficult, and the end of a cherished group or community brings pain. In Western society we often fail to properly attend to such matters, so a lot of grieving is sublimated only to erupt in other ways. An effective mentor will seek to attend to the suffering that comes with grief. Appropriate ways of celebrating the life of the community, of giving thanks for the gifts shared and received, and of honoring the participants are necessary highlights of graduations. But we also must not forget regrets and sadness, as well as the need to confess, forgive, and finally put aside the resentments we hold about past injuries.

Specific Skills for Guiding a Reflection Process

CHARTING TECHNIQUES

The techniques of tracking or charting a theological reflection can greatly affect the effectiveness of a seminar. Newsprint or a board on which to write can be a very helpful tool on which to track a reflection, although some groups work by allowing each participant to chart on their own notepads. What is important about a chart is that it keeps the group focused. It preserves information that may be needed later in the process and allows the participants both to see and hear key elements of the reflection.

It is important not to get bogged down in the charting. Sometimes it helps to chart in a way that is not linear (show diagrams of possibilities), such as the layout of a mandela, as shown below.

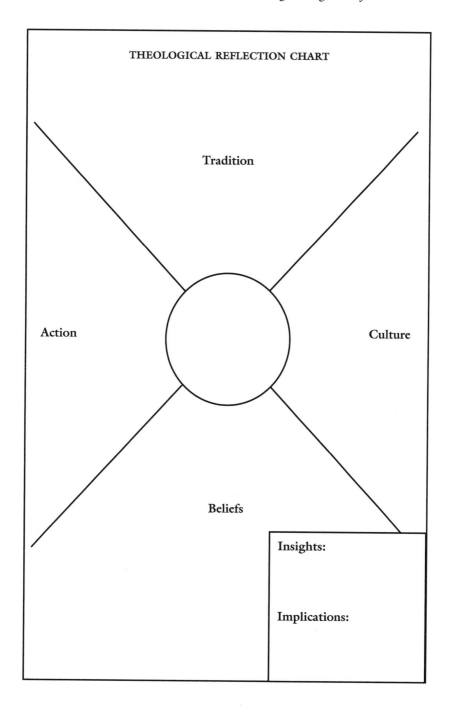

THEOLOGICAL REFLECTION CHART

Tradition

Action

Culture

Beliefs

Insights:

Implications:

Charting can also remind everyone of the purpose. It is very helpful at the very beginning to set aside a chart devoted to insights and possible implications. Insights may occur at any time. They are those magic moments when someone comes to a realization that has the potential for the future. Insights are those "Aha" moments of life. Sometimes we need others to help us recognize them. Writing them on a chart preserves and shares insights with the community of the seminar.

SHARING THE LEADERSHIP

The mentor or guide brings the skills and tools to a seminar, but the responsibility for learning belongs to everyone. Even the best mentor will falter. Sharing the leadership provides a number of benefits. First, others can help the group stay on track. Second, participants will learn the model and methods when it is their turn to lead. Third, and most important, there will be the joy of sharing what is learned, something that can then be celebrated and enjoyed by the entire seminar community.

CLOSING A REFLECTION

The techniques of ending a reflection are important because that is when the seminar takes time to reap the benefits of the exercise. It is extremely important to ask for what has been learned and to glean the insights so that everyone can share them and give thanks. It is also important at the close to acknowledge those who have made special contributions and to allow them to make a final comment.

AN EARLY CLOSE

There may be occasions when a reflection cannot be concluded and some major steps have not been reached. One way to deal with that is to save the charts and return to them at the next meeting. That may work, but often the group will shift in its mood, concern, and participants, and this will be difficult. Another way to conclude early is to bypass the steps that have not been completed and simply take a few moments to glean insights that may have occurred to the participants.

WHAT A THEOLOGICAL REFLECTION IS NOT

Finally, a word needs to be added to describe what a theological reflection is not. More is said about this in Chapter 15 on the ethics of theological reflection, but at this juncture it is important to note that our techniques of reflection are not appropriate to engage in problem-solving, psychological therapy, or converting others to a point of view. Thinking theologically may bring insights that respond to a problem, but that is not the purpose of the reflection. We hope that all we do brings healing and reconciliation, but theological reflection is not a diagnostic or prognostic tool, nor is it a regimen to cure something that is ailing, whether that be personal or communal. Finally, theological reflection is not an occasion to impose or manipulate change in other people. To be sure, any reflective activity may produce a decision to make changes, but a theological reflection itself should not be the only factor to determine what a change should be. In other words, those leading theological reflection need to remember that they are present as mentors who open the gateways to discovery rather than directors who determine a course of action.

USING THE SKILLS FOR REFLECTION IN OTHER EDUCATIONAL VENUES

First, theological reflections may be used to study all aspects of the theological enterprise. For instance, if there exists a desire to study hymnody, then the text from which to begin will emerge from the Church's hymnody. If one wishes to develop a better sense of prayer, then subjecting prayers to a theological reflection is an effective way of accomplishing this.

The second obvious situation in which theological reflection may be useful is when participants in a conflict are willing to gain insight into their situation. This is not a case of conflict management or resolution, although gaining insight may be a factor that will terminate a conflicted situation. What theological reflection can do to support persons or groups in conflict is to bring a modicum of acceptance and understanding that can produce a basis for developing a satisfying resolution.

Ranging more widely, however, the methods of theological reflection can be applied to learning in other disciplines. What we have described as theological reflection is nothing more than a creative method for structuring a seminar.

The Preparation of Mentors

Mentors are created or trained, not born. Some may have more personal and social skills and some may have quicker minds, but the skills of becoming a mentor depend upon adequate training. I like to compare this to becoming a pilot. Some possess natural skills to pilot an aircraft, but no one can do so without extensive preparation. That is also true for mentors or leaders of seminars. It is also true that some individuals may not be suited to become mentors.[2]

Requiring training is one thing; providing training that is effective is another. Training mentors is primarily a process of coaching while simultaneously providing sufficient relevant information. That information, however, is best learned if it is acquired close to the moment that makes it useful. Creating those moments is the heart of the training process. Like a pilot flying a plane, a future mentor needs to take hold of the situation and experience it. A trainer has the responsibility of keeping the venue safe, emotionally as well as physically, for training. Of course, the candidate must be willing to take the risk of not performing effectively before others.

What we are describing, of course, is the action/reflection approach to education, a method that insists on disciplined reflection as the path toward learning. That is the way most adults learn best, for most educators know that certain elements need to be present over time if an adult educational program is to be effective. Among these elements are these three:

- Education must make a difference. It's not just an academic exercise.
- An educational process must take seriously the contribution of the student. The student is part of the text.
- An educational process must treat participants as peers in a venture rather than passive partners to be molded.

Conclusion

Leading a seminar requires the skills of a mentor. Those skills can be acquired through practice under a competent coach. Another set of skills, those of a coach (being a trainer), are needed to teach others to lead seminars, but the two tasks—leading a seminar and training leaders for seminars—are closely related. Both are best achieved when an action/reflection process is used. That requires time to practice in a supportive environment. The process and the skills that can be learned in this way apply to multiple disciplines and are especially appropriate for theology.

2. The Education for Ministry program, from which the methods of theological reflection in this book developed, requires eighteen contact hours of training. Accreditation is not automatic, and a mentor must return for training no less than every eighteen months to maintain accreditation.

CHAPTER 15

The Ethics of Theological Reflection

The process of theological reflection in a small group can be very intense and may lead to life-changing decisions. In other words, theological reflection has the power to bring participants to decisions that may forever alter their lives. Of course, those personal decisions have implications for others as well; therefore, at this juncture it is time to consider the implications of theological reflection, something rarely discussed among theologians who are in the teaching professions or Christian educators. Engaging with others in a reflection that brings theological insights to the routines, as well as the inevitable changes through which we all live, has repercussions, some of them far-reaching. How we deal with them is a question of ethics. So is the fact that we intentionally establish venues for these insights to develop.

Respect for Differences

Bigotry seems made for religion—at least it is often among the most fervent believers that we find those who think most strongly that they have the answers for all times and for all people. We become bigots when we insist that we, and only we, have the only correct information and the proper perspective. Yet we, at least in the West, also tend to believe that it is not ethical among adults to impose a particular frame of mind or information on others. Our sense of individual freedom is paramount. A learning venue in which communications can flow depends upon the ability to suspend judgment at least long enough to hear clearly what is offered and taken seriously. A seminar has some of the characteristics of a family that hangs together, yet respects and loves the characteristics of its different members. Somehow a seminar must function to help its participants discard, at least temporarily, those human tendencies for self-protection to demand that everyone should follow the same path and accept the same assumptions. That need not mean, however, that we have abandoned our morals or our own well-established beliefs.

A primary ethic needed to work with others in a seminar setting is the decision to provide sufficient acceptance to all participants. That is not the same as agreement or support, but it does mean being present and listening. Making that choice is an ethical act, because it means that we govern ourselves in a seminar with a respect for the individual participants. That comes prior to performing any task, and it has its limitations.

Making Decisions

Arriving at a decision as a group or community is not easy unless a driving force has produced cohesion. That may be the force of fear that brings a nation together when under attack. It may also be the power of success, such as cheering for the home team when a score is made and rejoicing en masse in its victory. But when the impetus for cohesion is not so compelling, consensus is not so easily achieved.

Often we make group decisions by surrendering the decision to the leader or a subgroup given leadership responsibilities. That works well enough if a basic consensus and the trust that must accompany it are strong. Usually this is effective for large groups that must make decisions rapidly. For example, if the building is on fire, there exists a consensus that the leader, or for that matter anyone who notices the fire, can call for evacuation without debate or discussion. That is real power, and we also know that it is one to be abused only under the peril of punishment. And if a congregation is about to enjoy a church picnic and the group perceives that there exists an impending thunderstorm, the group will be happy to allow a small committee to organize an alternate location.

Major long-term or life-changing decisions that are not made in the face of life-threatening circumstances are another matter. Those may be debated and require time to emerge. That is why it frequently takes a long time to conclude decisions about social matters, such as taxes, or changes of social mores, such as how much nudity we can tolerate at the beach. A decision imposed from the top or concluded too quickly will bypass opposition. But that is a momentary victory, for all too often a relatively small yet determined subgroup can and will sabotage the entire effort. Our system of taxation, for instance, requires a consensus about the viability and importance of taxes. A minority of the population could turn the system into shambles, for there would not be sufficient courts to prosecute or jails to hold a truly determined large cadre of protestors. The same is true for enforcing standards of decency in matters of dress.

The result of this short meander in the world of social decisions is to emphasize that a group engaging in education, and especially in theological reflection, will function only if its members assent to the path to be followed. It may take time, but achieving a consensus is essential to the process, and imposing a structure strictly from the official leadership is an ethical violation. As so often when ethics are violated, ultimately the heavy hand does not carry the issue over the long haul.

A Consensus: What Is It?

A consensus means that there is sufficient agreement to proceed. It does not mean that all members of a group are overjoyed or would proceed down a certain avenue if left to their own choice. Most communities ultimately exist under a consensus, even if that consensus is no more than the willingness to live under autocracy. A community that does not exist with a modicum of consensus must either live under force, or the threat of force, or it must actually be incarcerated. Even then, however, the force of the community will find ways to express itself, sometimes at great risk to individual members.

A seminar is a micro-community, so an effective seminar requires a consensus to be reached. Achieving a consensus is an ethical as well as a procedural consideration. That is exceptionally important in determining the life of the seminar, for the insights of people in a seminar often have long-term, important consequences. If autocratic leadership thwarts the opportunity for a consensus to develop, the results will be rejected because no agreement was reached. For leadership to fail to work to a consensus is unethical. It will destroy group cohesiveness, and the results may prove to be disastrous.

Truthfulness

The old cliché "Honesty is the best policy" has more to commend it than its ethical value. It is good policy because honesty preserves that most important commodity, trust. Trust is a commodity because it must be earned. But it is an odd commodity. It cannot be sold, yet a climate of trust can be conveyed to and perceived by those who enter a seminar where trust exists. Trust is also a fragile commodity. Once lost, it is difficult to recover. Dishonesty is the great destroyer of trust, the kind of trust needed to maintain an effective learning venue, especially a seminar that depends upon its members to produce the learning opportunities.

Secrecy

J.R.R. Tolkien's trilogy *The Lord of the Rings* uses the motif of a ring that grants anyone wearing it invisibility. It is the ultimate invisible blanket, for it provides the opportunity to be invisible yet in plain sight. The stories that go with the ring range through four volumes of adventures, which, among other things, depict the power, influence, and consequences of the use of secrecy.[1] The hobbits only begin to use the ring when they are threatened. That is a noble purpose, but the use of the ring tends to make the user disagreeable. It reminds one a bit of the old advertisement for Crackerjacks, a sweetened popcorn creation: "The more you eat, the more you want." Secrecy is like that. The more you use it, the greater the desire and need to keep things cloaked. In other words, secrecy is the path to evil and self-destruction.

The consequences of secrecy have many negative implications. While secrecy can ensure protection from mischief and, in wartime, from destruction, the presence of secrecy invites mistrust and abuse. It invites those who hold the secrets to become tyrannical over those who are not knowledgeable. It is the morass for the growth of betrayals, gossip, whispers, and secret attempts to discover secrets—all the unfortunate attributes that accompany the games of spies and saboteurs,[2] as well as dalliances and office politics.

In educational matters secrecy may not lead to physical deaths as it might in war, but it can lead to personal and professional tragedies. In-

1. J.R.R. Tolkien, *The Hobbit, or, There and Back Again* (London: Allen & Unwin, 1984, © 1976).

2. It may be far afield but an interesting observation that the lack of secrecy may well be peace's greatest ally. Spies may cause havoc, but they may also avoid war. For instance, during the Cold War between the United States and Russia, Russian spies provided information that helped the Russians track American submarines. From this they realized that the United States was not seeking war, and they found it much more believable than official government pronouncements. On the other hand, American wiretaps of Russian naval maneuvers reassured the United States that Russian intentions were defensive in nature. Those realizations helped to bring detente, truly an example that maintaining secrecy is not always the best pathway to what we truly desire. Perhaps there is a lesson in this for our educational and administrative practices. The "water cooler" conversation where secrets slip may be more productive than is usually assumed.

evitably, it leads to a loss of that trust that is essential for discovery and learning, regardless of whether it is personal, social, or scientific.

Open Methods/Private Circumstances

Many small groups working in seminars adhere to an ethic of confidentiality. Confidentiality is about private circumstances—those aspects of life that belong to the individual and are usually best controlled by personal decisions. Of course, as we know, the right to confidentiality often does not extend to public figures. If a chief of state is ill, that fact affects an entire nation. It is not a confidential matter. So the question exists: How do we discern between public matters, which are kept secret only at the peril of losing the confidence of the community, and matters properly left confidential? In other words, where is the division between confidentiality and secrecy?

In the educational venue of the seminar, where confidential matters apply to the individuals involved and their immediate associates, the personal aspects of life are what is confidential. What should always be public are the purpose, process, procedures, membership, and leadership of the seminar. A seminar engaged in theological reflection is not a "secret society" with a "secret agenda." The texts, the methods, the aims, and the results should be open to public scrutiny. They do not have to be formally announced, but the information should be available to those who inquire.[3]

Confidentiality

One essence of a seminar engaged in a reflective process, especially theological reflection, is that the process engages the participants at a personal intellectual and emotional level. That cannot happen without appropriate self-revelation. To achieve a personal consideration of one's personal involvement with the subject under study in a seminar requires individual courage and community trust. One aspect of that trust is the knowledge that confidentiality is a normative characteristic of the group. Everyone needs to commit to maintaining confidentiality for the reflections to proceed in depth.

The ethics of confidentiality are important, but these need to be realistic and up front. Only those who are married, lawyers, physicians,

---

3. Please note that this ethic of openness is in juxtaposition to cults and special groups that hold participants to a pledge of secrecy. When secrecy abounds, it is more likely that the education is one of indoctrination rather than reflection.

some counselors, and clergy have legal as well as moral rights to maintain confidentiality. This protection does not extend to seminars that are part of an educational process. In other words, a group cannot engage in keeping confidential matters that are clearly illegal. Nor can group members maintain a stance that they will never tell when no protection exists that would prevent a subpoena and demand testimony before a jury about matters presented in a seminar. That may seem like a grave example, but it is important ethically that a mentor or leader not give assurances that cannot, in fact, be maintained.

The Open Book

The ethical stance, then, for a mentor or group leader, as well as for those who participate in a seminar, is the stance of the open book. A seminar is like a book to be studied. The information to be gleaned comes from the participants and what they bring. They are the primary texts, because they bring with them the stories of the past. Every member of a seminar has responsibility for her or his own learning, and everyone has responsibility for the effectiveness of the seminar. The process works best when maintaining an ethical learning venue is understood and supported by everyone present. To pursue the way of honesty is to treat the seminar like an open book, one in which private information will be left in the control of the individual, but public information will be there to be shared and learned by all who may be interested.

The Implications of Change

Learning has consequences, and learning in a seminar over an extended period of time can bring about significant opportunities for change. When one person changes, that has consequences on others—first the family, but then also associates, friends, and colleagues. Those engaged in a process of learning in a seminar setting have a responsibility to let others who may be affected have opportunities to be informed and even, when necessary, reassured.

One phenomenon I have observed over the years is the syndrome of the "absent spouse." That is the spouse who may have a certain sense of abandonment because the other person in the relationship is away once a week for a set period of time. When one person attends meetings once a week for several months, the spouse begins to wonder about these associations. It is important to provide occasionally, perhaps socially, perhaps by a presentation demonstrative of the work, to bring spouses or significant persons together so that they may develop a sense of what is taking place. The same factor also exists for some clubs that occasionally hold an inclusive event to remedy the uneasiness felt by the absent spouse.

The Effects on the Community

Finally, as we look to the community that may be affected by a seminar, it is important to remember that we do not act or change in isolation. Our decisions may be personal and relatively inconsequential, but they can and do affect other people. Sometimes a great host of persons are touched by what we do. As participants in a seminar learn and make decisions, the seminar membership has an ethical duty to provide an opportunity to examine how this might affect others.

We cannot avoid the factor of the consequences of our actions. What we do and what we fail to do have an effect on others. This factor has both positive and negative attributes. For instance, individuals as well as corporations contribute to pollution of the air, as the cumulative effect of auto exhausts demonstrates. But individuals as well as groups and institutions also produce benefits. In fact, we cannot estimate the consequences of our deeds with accuracy, but we can consider their effects. To do so is the only ethical stance, always recognizing that we are imperfect people in an imperfect world. That may temper our elation, but the joy returns when we recognize our imperfections and redeem them by learning from them. Through courage and a continual process of reflection the world is changed a little for the better.

Group Cohesion

As Christians we claim to focus on the truth, on openness, and on love. That needs to be kept in mind when we select our methods for bringing and maintaining group cohesion. It is easy to develop techniques that focus on breathing or on singing together and evoke emotional content as well as adding a message that provides a rational explication. But when this is done with a vow of secrecy about the methods employed, we are likely to encounter the possibility of abuse. It is also easy to involve people emotionally by leading them to divulge more than is appropriate. The processes of a seminar, the way it functions, and the methods that are used need to be public knowledge.

Finally, many groups claim to maintain secrecy or confidentiality, and that is sometimes used to urge that everything taking place in a seminar needs to remain there. There is a difference between confidentiality, which preserves personal data and information, and secrecy, which conceals techniques, methods, and points of view. Various sects and cults, Christian and other, have been known to use reflective techniques with immense success. They are the basic tools we employ to motivate people to perform sacrificial acts or mold them into successful teams. The same techniques are used by the military to mold soldiers, by fraternities and sororities to incorporate new members, and by church groups to produce conversions. Those are powerful educational processes that deserve to be treated carefully. Christian theologians—that means all of us—have a responsibility to demand an ethic governed by public oversight. A sure sign of misuse of reflective techniques is an insistence on secrecy. Another is the guiding dominance of a single leader. Reflective education is best led by a humble mentor, one who acts like a shepherd caring for a flock rather than a guru evoking sapient sentences. A shepherd lives with and learns from the flock.

CHAPTER 16

Reflection
The Creation of Power
in the Information Age

The Paradigm Shift

The phenomenon known as a "paradigm shift" has become a near cliché today. Thomas Kuhn wrote about this when he recognized paradigm shifts as a fundamental problem faced by our civilization.[1] It occurs when we begin to recognize that the information we discover puts well-honed assumptions into question. Usually there is resistance to such a shift of perspective, whether it occurs as a social phenomenon, a scientific discovery, or a personal event. In fact, a paradigm shift might be defined as the discovery of information that is so surprising that it is at first denied, sometimes vehemently so.

A good example of this denial of newfound reality was the encounter of Galileo with the Church when he announced that he could demonstrate that the universe really does not rotate around the earth. Another example that society rejected for a time was the theory of evolution, which suggested that human beings evolved from prior species. Still another was Albert Einstein's theory of relativity, which suggested that time and space are not constant in all places and in all circumstances. Einstein himself tended to reject some of its implications, namely, the notion that the universe could not be described in deterministic terms. The now famous quote "God does not play dice with the universe" expressed Einstein's difficulty in accepting the implications of his own theory of relativity.

---

1. Thomas S. Kuhn, *The Structure of Scientific Revolutions* (Chicago: University of Chicago Press, 1970).

The failure to accept a major shift in our perception of the universe can have devastating consequences. For instance, the Swiss watchmakers owned the rights to produce digital timepieces. When they failed to recognize that the public might accept this innovation with enthusiasm, they ceded the rights to produce digital watches to Japan. In a few years the ancient Swiss tradition of producing fine mechanical watches was decimated, because inexpensive and very accurate digital watches captured most of the market for timepieces. On an even more mundane level, in 1964 I chanced to tell my European cousins about keeping bread frozen as a means of preventing waste and assuring a steady supply in the house. They loved their French bread and were aghast at the thought, certain that frozen bread would surely become a mushy mess when defrosted. Ten years later their paradigm about bread had shifted. They now possessed their own freezer stocked with, among other things, loaves of French bread.

The Creation of Power

The creation of power ultimately depends on the ability to develop techniques that permit human capacity to exercise control over the environment as well as over human beings. New techniques, however, come by developing new information. This is the power of discovery, the power of developing new technology as well as new understandings about that technology. Simply engaging in new activities is not discovery itself, however. If one goes on and repeats the same activity over and over again without reflection, nothing is learned. The title of this book developed because of the recognition that information combined with knowledge—the ability to derive meaning about what we learn—is the elementary step in the creation of power. Thus the two elements of reflection are information or data and the knowledge and ability to make use of the data we acquire. What truly makes this power useful, however, is the ability to give it meaning and purpose. Meaning and purpose are spiritual categories rooted in theology. That is why theological reflection offers the opportunity to create spiritual power required in an information age, one that continually explodes with new data, insights, and techniques.

Power Shifts

Alvin Toffler recognized the increasing rapidity of change in his popular book that suggested that people in the latter half of the twentieth century were in shock over this.[2] He pursued his thesis and eventually

2. Alvin Toffler, *Future Shock* (New York: Random House, 1970).

concluded that the information age, which we had entered with computer and electronic technology, was doing more than changing the balance of power. With access to information increasingly available, the computer age had a democratizing effect. Totalitarian governments found it increasingly difficult to restrict information to and among their population, a control necessary to retain power. One by one these regimes began to topple. But a decade later Toffler noted that, while these changes were significant, what was really occurring was a shift in the nature of power itself.[3] Power no longer always belonged to the strongest or the wealthiest; it was accruing to the smartest, those who possess information, can make use of it, and can communicate to others rapidly and accurately. This shift is more than a redirection of power between individuals, institutions, or nationalities. The real shift is hidden, because the relationships of force, wealth, and knowledge are shifting. Toffler calls this shift both dangerous and exhilarating.[4] The danger has been aptly demonstrated when dedicated purveyors of terror destroy large buildings and kill thousands. The exhilaration, or perhaps better stated, the awful awe is manifested when we can all watch it happen in real time on our television. Just how this affects spirituality, and what we might accomplish with theological reflection that develops our Christian spirituality, is the crucial conclusion, which we now strive to attain.

Power from Force

Toffler's thesis is that for much of history the dominant power in the world was the use of force, the force of arms and brute strength. When force dominates, conquest is paramount. The control of territory is the chief value. To this end castles and fortifications were constructed, as was the Great Wall of China, with a view to exercising power through force and owning territory.

Economic Power

The nature of power shifted as the mercantile era developed during the Renaissance. Financial power rose to the forefront. Money purchased

---

3. Alvin Toffler, *Power Shift: Knowledge, Wealth, and Violence at the Edge of the 21st Century* (New York: Bantam Books, 1990).
4. Ibid., 464.

armies, and commercial interests drove the colonial spirit. Financial power became the bastions, and our great cities were soon populated with edifices devoted to the world of commerce and finance—banks, insurance companies, and exchanges replaced fortresses and cathedrals as the new monuments of the mercantile era. They clustered together in large groups to facilitate exchanges. The ability to understand finances became the new wizardry that powered nations. To be sure, many governments did not make the shift, and even now there remains a tendency to value territory over commerce, something that explains some of the civil strife that continues to plague nations as they seek to regain control over their lands (gain independence). What has changed today is that money can no longer be safely held like gold in a vault. Money has become information, or as John Naisbitt calls it, "information in motion."[5]

The Information Age

By the last quarter of the twentieth century, with the advent of the electronic age, the nature of power shifted once again. Now money became information in electronic format. The power to make things happen resides among those who possess access to information and the ability to manipulate, store, transmit, and exchange it throughout the world in a matter of seconds. Today I can launch an auction from my home in Tennessee through computers in California that link me to a buyer in Australia who may be viewing a photo of the item for sale through a computer in Europe. The capacity to manipulate data has made the playing field accessible virtually everywhere. That is what makes what I describe possible, and it is also what makes horrendous acts like a well-organized suicidal act of warfare led by people in a remote country available to those who are most angry.

We are still in the midst of adapting to the power shift that we loosely call the "information age." With each shift in power our institutions have adapted. Some have disappeared (pressing soldiers into service, once done by force or conscription, was done by financial emoluments, and is now achieved by recruitment and motivation). New institutions have developed. The money-changer in the temple became the banker, and today we are fast developing online services to handle financial transactions via electronic transfers.

---

5. John Naisbitt, *Megatrends: Ten New Directions Transforming our Lives* (New York: Warner Books, 1982) 91.

Religion and the Power Shift

The shift in power has affected all religious establishments and has caused some of the very worst symptoms of denial associated with major paradigm shifts. Regressive and blunt uses of the forces available to various religions have been used to forestall the changes. Where it has been possible, governmental forces have been enlisted to sustain conservative efforts. In other places powerful groups intent on maintaining earlier values have entered the political fray and sought to influence government. That has occurred across religious lines, among Christians and non-Christians alike, and continues to be a factor. Those opposing globalization, disparate and in disagreement with each other, are an example. So are those who advocate a return to nature and a "simpler life." To be sure, there are reasons for the growing opposition to technology, just as there were reasons to oppose industrialization in the eighteenth and nineteenth centuries. Like the genie of industry, the genie of technology is not always a benevolence to be welcomed.

The Church and the Power of Knowledge

I am grateful to Margaret Wheatley's provocative book on the relationship of science and our emerging social matrix for posing Michael Talbot's question, "What if information is the basic ingredient of the universe?"[6] Perhaps that is where the information age will lead us: that all matter and energy are merely information to be arranged and re-arranged, configured and reconfigured. This notion then describes a universe that is at once ineffable yet touchable, divine and yet incarnate, not unlike the spiritual dimension of our existence we call the spiritual self or the soul. It would describe a universe that evokes creation out of its information encounters as bits gather, mass, form, and interact to become sensible entities.

The Church as a Center for Finding Meaning

Often religious education has failed to provide a venue and a process for finding meaning. Perhaps this explains the following:

> The reason America's churches and religious institutions may seem emptier these days is that in the last decade, the proportion of Americans who said they have no religious preference doubled, from 7 percent

6. Margaret J. Wheatley, *Leadership and the New Science* (San Francisco: Berrett Koehlers, 1992).

to 14 percent. . . . Yet this decline does not necessarily reflect an increasing secularization in America . . . for evidence indicates that "the new religious dissenters have distanced themselves from the churches, not from God. . . . The majority of adults who prefer no religion continue to believe in God and an afterlife." While these Americans clearly reject being labeled "religious," they still consider themselves "spiritual."[7]

With the information explosion has come a destabilization of assumptions about the spiritual aspects of life, those aspects that govern the totality of human experience, give them meaning, and provide a sense of purpose. People have sought to reclaim or find their spiritual values with all sorts of techniques, including those provided by established religions. I submit that while prayer is a part of what is necessary, it is not sufficient itself. What brings meaning, certainly within a Christian context, is the opportunity to engage in a disciplined pattern of theological reflection, pursued within the bosom of a Christian community that is small enough to bond but large enough to provide the energy that comes with different points of view.

Spirituality

The *Encyclopedia of Theology* provides eighteen pages of text under the entry "spirituality."[8] By its very length this encyclopedia demonstrates the possibility that the word "spirituality" is a concept simultaneously enriched by too much meaning and yet impoverished by a lack of clarity. For some, spirituality is only a Christian concept, which is the way the *Encyclopedia of Theology* tends to treat it. For others, a "spiritual person," someone who shows spirituality, is someone who conveys a certain sense of serenity and wisdom. Consequently, someone who is scattered, thoughtless, noisy, and foolish is considered as not spiritual. Still others equate spirituality with the artifices of mediums, soothsayers, and palm readers. Finally, some Christians look for the spiritual in the gifts of the spirit and believe that true spirituality is found in emotional ecstasy that may be exhibited through speaking in tongues, uninhibited dancing, weeping, or even laughter.

7. Michael Hout and Claude S. Fischer, "Losing Religion, but Not Spirituality," *American Sociological Review* (April 2002).

8. Karl Rahner, ed., *Encyclopedia of Theology* (New York: Seabury Press, 1975) 1623–1641.

In the context of creating spiritual power for the age of information, however, we might consider spirituality in a way that is somewhat different from the popular attributes frequently connected with the word "spiritual." A fecund spirituality may be found in the serenity of meditation and the cloister, but it may also be found in the chaotic and unbounded. Moreover, a destructive spirit may be founded in the quietness of rational tranquility as well as in the extremes of emotional fervor.

Spirituality expresses something about the human condition. The spirit we demonstrate may be loving or abominable. It may be creative or destructive. It may be self-sacrificing or self-serving. It may even be some combination that is neither perfect goodness nor unmitigated evil, because spirituality actually is a way of talking about our totality, an aspect of human existence that is most clearly depicted by the word "soul." Our spirituality is a product of our soul. This is not an ineffable addition to our humanity that will waft away like a breeze at death but rather an ineffable expression of the totality of our human existence. While we cannot pin it down, we can identify attributes of the soul as they are expressed by major characteristics, namely, our physical presence (yes, body language counts), our rational or thinking expressions, and our emotional presence. Spirituality is about these three aspects of our souls, and perhaps more, but at least about these three. When we engage in theological reflection, we seek to develop our spiritual life, and as Christians, the spiritual life we seek is defined by our faith in Christ.

Simple reflective activities are a way of gathering information about the world and ourselves. When we derive the meaning of the information we obtain, we begin to seek relationships. Relationships may begin with information about us and our surroundings, then develop into human associations, and finally seek the transcendent. That process is always a theological reflection because it ultimately aspires to the transcendent. It may, of course, not be Christian. Yet those who find life worthwhile do seek a way to express what they find of value in life through their acts. They have value because they have worth to others. For that reason they find meaning for their lives, and that meaning has the potential to extend to the transcendent and divine. That is the very essence of ministry, for to be of worth to others gives life significance and extends our significance beyond the immediacy of time and place. Perhaps, however, that is only another correlate to the biblical observation that to love one's neighbor is to love God.

Asking the Right Questions

Earlier within these pages I described the process of theological reflection—telling our story, gathering insights, and deciding on implications—and I emphasized that questions that begin with who, what, where, and when are preferable because they expose information. Once information is on the table, answers to questions around method (how) and purpose (why) may become self-evident. I also suggested that questions about how and why are not very helpful because we tend to answer them defensively. Asking the right question in the right way is also a question of timing. Now, as we approach a conclusion, it is time to reclaim the opportunity to ask about method and purpose (how and why), not as an aid in reflection but as a step forward in spirituality. Unfortunately, however, we use the interrogatives "how" and "why" rather glibly in social interactions.

The Total Question: How . . . ?

"How are you?" "I'm fine." This is a typical exchange that gathers very little information but is really no more than a polite and customary greeting. Yet when pursued, a question like "How are you?" can quickly become very complex and very personal. It is complex because if I truly take stock of how I am, I would need to take into consideration all aspects of my physical health, mental state, and emotional stability. What I seek to point out here is that "how" questions really point to the totality of our being, and that is what I would define as our spiritual state.

To use another example, if we ask, "What did you do to achieve . . . ?" the answer can take us step by step through a process. But if we ask, "How did you do that?" we are really asking about the totality of the act, so that it may be proper to delineate the steps but also to attest to the origin of how we learned those steps.

"How" questions, when pressed, are also very personal. To answer fully a question such as "How did you come to write this text?" I would need to reveal my own biography. I would need to talk about my teachers, the influence of my family, my failures, and my successes; in short, I would be attempting to articulate the totality of my existence, although, of course, that could never be achieved.

The Ultimate Question: Why . . . ?

When we initiate a question with "why," we are asking the question of purpose. It is the ultimate question that points directly to the issue of faith. All too often when things go wrong we ask, "Why did that happen?" Most often we seek something or someone to blame, and those who are quizzed go on the defensive.

Pressed to their limit, questions that begin with "why" force us to consider our deepest affirmation. Our answers reveal the God or idols we worship. To be sure, what we worship may not be the God Almighty of Christ Jesus, but our answer does describe what is important to us, the little gods or idols that we tend to worship, even when we maintain a Christian identity. In other words, when we ask "why" with intensity, we are truly asking the profound and personal spiritual question of faith.

Theological Reflection as a Spiritual Quest

Reflection is an analytical process, but theological reflection is a spiritual quest, because it leads to a consideration of faith that is in turn demonstrated by commitments. Whenever reflective questions are probed, we are engaging a theological dimension. The responses, of course, may be diverse. They are not necessarily Christian answers, nor even properly religious, in the sense of an organized religion, but they are a linkage to something greater than the individual, something that motivates and drives, something that provides the power to proceed and move to new things.

Spirituality and the Creation of Power

In this manner our theological reflections as spiritual exercises are the tools by which to create power in an age of information that desperately seeks to make sense and find purpose amidst an abundance of information. When our reflections emphasize a redemptive and caring relationship, we discover a creative spiritual power. That spiritual energy is what energizes, brings hope, motivates charity, promotes stewardship, and exhibits the attributes of divine love that we associate with the ministry of Jesus, his selfless sacrifice on our behalf, the renewal of Easter, and the appearance of the Risen Lord.

Perhaps a symbol of Easter is to be found in the observation that our times require "high tech/high touch."[9] John Naisbitt suggests that our technology produces a greater desire to be with one another. I would suggest that this is also to find Christ anew in one another, an Easter moment. Nightclubs, large crowds at sport events, and crowded

9. Naisbitt, *Megatrends,* 39ff.

shoppers in the mall may occur because people sense the need for others. But none of these satisfy the hunger for proximity like a small group working closely together to discover and express what gives life meaning in a personal way. Probably the Church's first apostles demonstrated how a small band can come together and be so changed that they in turn change the world. There have been many other such bands. Some came together to survive, others were scientists in a laboratory making important discoveries, and others were people like the founding fathers of the United States who brought forth a new and different nation. When the creative force of an insightful small group merges a motley crew into a team, somehow they weld together a powerful entity. Theological reflection, well organized, done with humility, prayer, and loving concern, is a method to develop that power. It can become a transforming power, one much needed in an age that is almost overwhelmed by changes, competing forces, a developing technological expertise, and an overabundance of data.

This transforming power is the power of wisdom, something that cannot be learned through coaching or lectures. Wisdom is discovered from life's pilgrimage, but not everyone finds it. Sometimes that path is arduous. Sometimes it is frightening. Sometimes it is enjoyable. Sometimes it is exhilarating. Without reflection, however, it is not sufficient to discover wisdom. When we achieve wisdom, it is more satisfying and powerful than owning vast possessions, controlling the world, having the applause of masses of people. It is the wisdom which links us to the saints and the ages and which we as Christians disclose most clearly in our love of God known through Christ Jesus. That process of discovery is the domain of a Spirit that is Holy.

APPENDICES

Introduction

A Word Concerning Methods of Theological Reflection

The methods in the Appendix depend upon the four-source model and the outline for the process of reflection presented earlier. These methods are ways of engaging in a focused conversation. They are not procedural recipes; to treat them in that manner misses the point. They originated in the careful observation of productive conversations and notes made to identify when conversations did not provide an opportunity to enjoy the joy of discovery.

Technical Preparation

1. It may be helpful to prepare certain graphics before beginning a theological reflection. These may be done on an erasable board, on large pieces of paper that may be viewed by the participants, or even on a computer screen when participants are not in the same room. I have found that a plastic-covered wallpaper over a large area works well. With washable markers, it can be used for years at little expense.

2. Some aspects of a reflection do not need to be retained before the group for very long, but it helps to have them posted while the group is pondering the next step. Other aspects need to be kept throughout the reflection. Those vary and are indicated in the descriptions given for each method.

3. The goal of a reflection is the discovery of insights and the identification of their implication. These do not always come neatly at the end. Often there are "Ah" moments in the midst of the conversation. Therefore, it is advised that before the reflection process begins, an area be devoted to insights and implications. They can be noted as they occur

so that the ideas will not be lost in the wake of subsequent discussions. In addition, posting an area of paper or a board for insights and implications reminds participants that there are a purpose and a goal to attain.

4. When a reflection must be cut short, asking for insights is a good way to close. Often even an incomplete conversation can produce significant occasions for learning from which insights may be gleaned.

5. While there is a sequence to the reflection process, we do not necessarily think sequentially. It can be helpful to post the various areas of reflection so that they are always visible to everyone. When someone offers something out of sequence, accept it, put it in its proper place, and then return to the sequence you were following. This will honor the offering but keep the group from straying into a nonproductive jumble of ideas.

6. Some people must speak to know what they think (extrovert); others must think before they can speak (introvert). It is easy for the extroverts to overwhelm those who need an opportunity to gather their thoughts. Even a minute or two of silence can be very helpful. Do not hesitate to provide time to contemplate.

7. When dealing with feelings, some may need support to identify their feelings. It can be very helpful to remember that, like primary colors red, blue, and yellow, mad, glad, sad, and afraid are the primary hues of our emotions. Usually when someone begins a phrase with "I feel that . . . ," what follows will be a thought or opinion rather than a feeling. One way to help someone beyond this kind of expression is to ask, "What did you feel underneath what you have just expressed?"

8. It may be elementary, but it is important to thank those who make offerings from their lives as occasions for theological reflection.

9. Ultimately, a theological reflection is most productive and creative when we can trust those who are with us, when we are free to explore "outside the box," and when we enjoy the confidentiality that permits us to reveal what is precious, appropriate in the context, and ultimately significant.

10. Techniques for creating metaphors. Creating metaphors is best achieved as something that is fun. Brainstorming is a great way to create a number of metaphorical images quickly. The key is to let the ideas flow without evaluation or censorship. One way to do this is to give a group a limited time, say five minutes, to create as many metaphors as possible. The speed of creation should only be limited by someone's ability to jot the metaphors down, preferably on a chalkboard or piece of newsprint that all can see.

Metaphors are images, and, technically speaking, they are not the same as similes. However, one way to help a group brainstorm for new metaphors is best done when a story has been told. The question to pose is: What is a picture, image, or metaphor that describes the story? What do you see? What do you smell, feel, hear, and sense in the story that is best evoked by this image?

11. Brainstorming. Brainstorming is a useful technique to develop many ideas quickly. Sometimes we need to warm up by brainstorming something silly like: How many different ways do you think you can use an undergarment? Limit the time to, say five minutes, with the ground rule that nothing will be critiqued, explained, or examined until the five minutes have passed. It is also helpful to take a moment, perhaps as long as two or three minutes, to be quiet and so serve as an opportunity to gather emotional, mental, and spiritual resources for the task.

After a brainstorming session concludes, offer to clarify what is confusing, select the useful ideas, and discuss what can be used. The process should be fun and energizing. Once a warm-up is completed, use the technique to develop a number of ideas that may be considered at a later time. Usually a group will agree fairly quickly that one or two ideas evoke best something useful for the ongoing conversation.

Inclusivity: The Bouncing Ball

Working in a small group sometimes means that some are more prone to speak than others. One way to help open the gates for everyone to speak is for the mentor or leader to speak first, then to toss (perhaps symbolically) permission to speak to someone else in the group by name. That person may decide to pass or to seize the opportunity. Regardless of the choice, that person has the task of selecting and bouncing the ball to someone else in the group who has yet to speak. This continues until everyone has had an opportunity. Usually, if someone passed up an opportunity early, it is important to check with that person before concluding the exercise.

A ball of yarn or string can be used with this exercise. In that case the ball is unwound as it moves from person to person. Participants hold the yarn at the point where it came to them so that eventually a net is formed. When the exercise concludes, the net helps to define graphically the linkage between all the participants. It also links everyone and can become a graphic to demonstrate how we are related to one another.

Our Life: A Text for Theological Reflection

When Adam and Even bit of the fruit of the tree of life, they were suddenly aware of their nakedness. With this act, described in the Book of Genesis, it may be said that the process of reflection has begun. The first steps leading to knowing God begin with this self-reflection of our vulnerability.

One place to begin theological reflection, therefore, is with our lives, with our activities. These are the most basic texts from which we can learn. Books and instructors bring us the world outside ourselves, but ultimately all that we learn is part of our experience. Our lives, therefore, are the primary text from which we learn about ourselves and the world we inhabit.

But life is large. When we look in the mirror, we see only a small part of ourselves—that part of the image in the mirror on which our eyes focus. The complexity of life and the fact that we always see through a glass both dim and distort. When we engage in theological reflection that begins with activities of our lives, it is essential to narrow the focus sufficiently so that we can reflect and learn something useful. It is equally essential to involve others in reflection so that we may correct for the distortions that inevitably occur when we are alone with our ruminations.

The method described in this Appendix lays out a way to proceed with a process of reflection that is best done in the community of a small group, led by a mentor who understands the process. That mentor can also pay attention to how a group works and how its life develops; however, the essence of the process is that all participants are able to have a share in the development, direction, and outcome of the seminar.

To facilitate this presentation of a complex process, various aspects are presented as a series of steps. The text in italics is a commentary on the steps that can help the group and its guide to overcome obstacles and difficulties that may arise.

Prerequisites

1. A theological reflection takes place best in a community that has developed a climate of trust as well as some norms for working together. To begin the reflection, someone—a presenter—must agree to present an event in his or her life that can be the basis for the reflection process.

2. It is very difficult to reflect very effectively as events occur. During the course of an event we focus on action and response. This requires reflection but not at the level of theological reflection, which comes later as we seek to uncover the meaning of what has happened. Consequently, it is important that an event selected for theological reflection be closed. We can learn from the event, but we can no longer go back to it and "fix" it or alter the situation. It is over and done with, except as an occasion for learning.

3. We may be lured to reflect on intense and dramatic events in our lives as an important focus for learning, but often we can learn more about our faith and ourselves when we concentrate on mundane events. The commonplace events of our lives may even seem trite, yet they may be found to contain all the richness of faith when they are examined, an experience all the more powerful because it demonstrates that faith is connected to the ordinary and does not require the extraordinary as proof.

It is important to remember that a theological reflection is not a debate with points to be scored. It is not a solution to a problem. It is not a course of therapy, and it is not an academic exercise. Theological reflection is a meaningful conversation that leads to insights about the present and opens possibilities for the future within a context of learning Christian theology.

Beginning a Reflection from Personal or Internal Sources

Personal sources for reflection originate in two areas of life: what we do and what we believe. Thus far we have emphasized that we learn a great deal when we reflect on the actions we take. The first method, therefore, originates with things that we do.

Part I—Beginning with a Text from Life's Experience

Preliminary Step: Someone may have been asked to prepare for this in advance. If the group is cohesive and people are free with one another, someone may volunteer to offer an initial story from which the reflection may begin.

Step 1. Someone in the group relates an event from which they might learn. The event should be reasonably short to relate, not more than ten minutes, and it should be concluded. This is not an event that can be revisited and continued. The event should not be a problem to be solved. It is not an issue to be pursued, nor should it seek a therapeutic answer.

The metaphor or image at the center is a symbolic way to represent the group's interpretation of the stories that were told. The key to telling a story is to select something that is concluded and relatively short. Tell the story— what happened; where and when did it happen; who was involved? If there is hesitancy, perhaps someone can do an "interview." The group may assist with this. A consensus should develop about the moment to select before proceeding.

Step 2. Identify the core element of the story. Perhaps one particular moment was more electrifying than others were. There may be several moments upon which to focus. Select one that both the group and the presenter sense is vital.

Step 3. Examine the moment and be clear about what it is; then ask the presenter to identify what feelings were present. Too many different feelings indicate that the event is not sufficiently focused. While feelings are complex, it may be easier to begin with a basic four—mad, sad, glad, and afraid. Avoid accepting statements that begin with "I feel that . . ." What usually follows is an opinion or judgment rather than a feeling or emotion. It is helpful to list the feelings on a board so that everyone can retain and work with what is expressed.

Step 4. Ask the presenter to express the thoughts that accompanied the feelings. These may be entered on a board next to the feelings to which they are attached.

It is helpful to write down the thoughts and feelings on a board so that everyone can see them.

Step 5. Now open up the process for the group to participate. Has anyone experienced these same thoughts and feelings, perhaps with very different kinds of events from the one that was presented? Offer people three to five minutes to relate their experiences.

Note to the mentor and the group: Some people have difficult relating an event, or they may present an event that is not concluded. Sometimes this is evident in the story itself. At other times the signs are subtle. Some indications that this will be difficult exist:

1. When the story becomes a series of stories or saga. When this happens you may wish to ask the presenter of the story to tell only a portion of the saga and to focus on a segment that has been concluded.

2. When the presenter has analyzed the story and is ready to provide answers to the next steps before they are reached. This is a sign that the presenter has a high stake in this story, and anxiety is running high, since the narration may have direct implications.

3. When a person tells about an event, often about an event that occurred to someone else, and has difficulty focusing on relating something in which there is personal involvement.

Corrective action: Sometimes a story must be abandoned. At other times it is possible to guide the presenter to a focus. One way to achieve this is to use the technique of an interview. Ask questions that begin with who, what, where, and when to elicit the information. Perhaps such presenters could be asked to take a moment of silence, think about the experience, put themselves in it again, and then describe what they hear, see, smell, taste, feel.

Part II—Moving beyond the Personal Experience

Brainstorm some ideas and record on a board or on newsprint images or metaphors that the thoughts and feelings evoked by the core event evoked. Everyone in the seminar may participate in this. After the energy subsides, take some time to ponder the results. Perhaps a specific image will be received with enthusiasm. Select the one that is the most appealing and full of energy for the group.

Place the metaphor or image at the center of a large piece of paper or on a board. The format on the next page suggests how to prepare the area on which to record the reflection.

Step 6. Exploring the Metaphor. Chapter 13 offers a theological interrogatory, questions to ask that explore the theological dimensions. Ask as many of the questions as may seem appropriate and record the group's responses.

This is a theological exploration of the experiences of the group. These questions may be posed using the technical language of theology, or they may be posed by using common phrases.

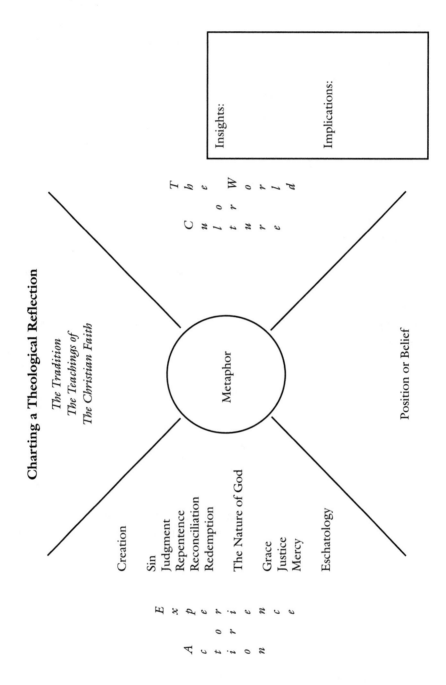

Charting a Theological Reflection

The Tradition
The Teachings of
The Christian Faith

Creation

Sin
Judgment
Repentence
Reconciliation
Redemption

The Nature of God

Grace
Justice
Mercy

Eschatology

Exploration
Acteriionmen

Culture
The
Wiorld

Metaphor

Position or Belief

Insights:

Implications:

Example 1: One might ask the group what doctrine of creation is found in the image or metaphor. One might also ask this in a nontechnical way with the question "What does the world of this metaphor look like?"

Example 2: One might ask where sin is found in a particular image or metaphor. One might also ask: Where do things go wrong? Where is there destruction and evil?

Step 7. The tradition of theology may now be addressed. One way to narrow the field is to seek stories, accounts, or statements from the Christian tradition that relate to the metaphor. This relationship may be in support of the metaphor or may raise questions about it. If possible, read the passage that may seem appropriate or find a way to make the information come alive to the participants. Sometimes several passages need to be examined before one can be found to study. It is important to select one item to explore.

Biblical passages may be very useful for this step, and a number of them may occur to members of the group. It is important to select one to explore in detail. While this means that many interesting paths cannot be pursued, it does allow some in-depth exploration of a passage and its relationship to what people in the group have experienced.

Step 8. The world outside our experience is a vast domain. Sometimes we define it as culture, but even that may be too large. Select a vignette from culture to explore and ask: "What does the world (culture) say to the metaphor we are examining?"

Note: It is important not to make culture into the "bad actor" but to recognize that the culture(s) we inhabit hold many values and that some of these are intimately connected with Christian values. It may be helpful to narrow the focus in the reflection to what culture says from a specific standpoint, such as that of the media, the theater, politics, the military, etc.

Step 9. Now comes a time to make comparisons. Let the discussion be freewheeling. What are the contrasts? Where is there agreement? What questions does the reflection bring to mind at this point?

Step 10. Examining personal beliefs can be very productive. Now is the time for people to express their personal ideas. The more trust, the more participants will feel free to express their thoughts without fear of reproof.

Note: This may be a time of disagreement between participants. It can also be an occasion for discovering that what we believe and what we do as well as what our faith says to us may not be congruent. Expressing personal beliefs in this climate can lead to insights.

Step 11. Now comes a time to identify what may have been learned. Insights may have occurred throughout the reflective conversation. If they are noted as the conversation proceeds, this is the time to highlight these insights.

Note: We find that this kind of group discussion frequently leads to delayed occasions for insights. The stimulation of the community may touch off a continued rumination that requires time to distill. Consequently, it may be helpful to ask at subsequent meetings if participants have had any new ideas occur to them based upon earlier work.

Step 12. Consequences: Insights are nice, but they make little difference unless we decide to act in a different manner. This is a time to explore the implications of what was learned. It is also a time to consider the implications that may be in this for others. For instance, if a specific course of action seems indicated, then the implications will probably affect others.

Christian Tradition as a Launching Point for Reflection

The mode of theological reflection most familiar to faithful Christians usually begins with a text that proclaims the faith in a way that strikes a chord. Christians most often begin their journey of reflection from a biblical passage or from a document inspired by the Bible. Hymns, prayers, sermons, and creeds—all these may serve as launching points for a period of reflection. The Bible thus is the most important and the most used source document.

Christian sources offer a wide panoply of material from which to reflect. Moreover, the documents are themselves complex. A reflection must have a focus, and for this reason the first step is to select a passage, story, or pericope from which to begin. That might be a section of Scripture, a hymn, a vignette from Church history, a statement from a creed or confession of faith, a prayer, or writings from important Church figures of the past.

Step 1. Review with care the portion of theological tradition you wish to use as the basis for reflection. If it is a Bible passage, you may wish to read it aloud and, if available, to read it in more than one translation.

Step 2. Identify what you know about the text that has been selected. When was it prepared? Who was the author? What was the historical context? If it is biblical and parallel texts exist, how do different translations handle the passage?

Step 3. Identify the focal passages or passage of the text. What is it striving to communicate with the most energy? If there are several passages that seem important, select the one that is of the most interest to the group. What is the core issue in the passage? What thoughts and feelings might have been evoked in the characters of the passage or for the author who wrote the passage?

Step 4. Ask the theological questions deemed to be applicable to this passage.

Example: Where do you find judgment in this passage? Or, what in this passage causes someone to take notice that something is amiss with the world to which the passage speaks?

Step 5. Bring in the world around us. What in the world or culture around us supports or contrasts with the core of the passage?

Step 6. See an event in your life that somehow corresponds or connects to the passage you are studying. Can you identify an event in your life that evoked some of the feelings and thoughts that were evoked in Step 3?

Step 7. What are your beliefs about this passage? What do you believe about how this text and the world relate to each other? What do you think is the theological value of this passage as it connects with the world and with your personal life?

Step 8. What insights have occurred to you during this reflection or that now come to you as you take time to meditate on the conversation that has taken place?

Step 9. Consequences: What will you do with what you have learned? How will it affect other people? What assistance or support do you need to pursue the insights and decisions you are making?

Reflecting on Personal Beliefs

Beliefs, creeds, and affirmations as beginning points for theological reflection are the most difficult entry into the process of theological reflection. There are few things more perilous than beginning with belief, because we tend to hold what we truly believe as something sacred. To offer a firmly held belief for reflection is to offer ourselves to change, perhaps to admit that we are mistaken. While most people value the ability to admit error, few of us do so easily and graciously. We have to be convinced, and we tend to resist the confrontation that will evoke the necessity for change.

This method of reflection may be used to understand the different positions held by members of a seminar group or community. There needs to be a consensus about process and a commitment of respect and commitment, but there can be real differences among group members about social, political, religious, and ethical matters. This is one way of giving such differences consideration and learning from one another without totally disrupting the community.

A change of belief is a conversion and so not to be taken lightly. Because personal beliefs are precious, a reflection that begins with someone's belief needs to be handled very gently. To protect participants, the group needs to adhere to some guidelines, such as:

a) The freedom to say no. No one is to be pressured to offer his or her belief as the focus for a reflection.

b) Trust is an important factor. Do not initiate such a conversation with people who do not know and trust one another.

c) Beliefs are offered for theological scrutiny rather than for critique, negation, or vilification. When someone offers a belief for reflection, that belief must be honored and the person must be treated as a peer who is not to be judged.

d) The purpose of a reflection that focuses on beliefs is to look at the theology that the belief reveals and how that theology measures to others' experience and the Christian tradition.

Procedure

PERSONAL AND INTERIOR SOURCES

Step 1. A topic is selected upon which to begin the reflection. It should be a topic of interest, one about which there will be different opinions among the members of the group. It may, or course, be controversial. Record the different beliefs on a board or newsprint.

Note: Anyone who offers his or her belief should not be asked to defend it. Any explanation that is asked should only go to clarity about the belief itself.

Step 2. Continuing in the personal dimension of the beliefs expressed, each person is asked: When have you experienced strong feelings around this belief? What produced these feelings? What, if anything, did you do about them?

EXTERNAL SOURCES

Step 3. The larger world must deal with the same topics. Brainstorm the responses of our culture in regard to the topic identified in Step 1.

Step 4. Chart on newsprint or a board how the Christian tradition responds to the topic identified in Step 1. Be specific with passages from Scripture or other examples. If the group selects recent Church pronouncements, you may wish to examine how these have been influenced by Christian values and by cultural values that are or are not necessarily of Christian origin.

Step 5. Compare and contrast the various sources. Where is there agreement? Where is there support?

THEOLOGICAL ANALYSIS

Step 6. Ask questions from the theological interrogatory in Chapter 13. Some questions to raise might be:

—What kind of a world does this reflection reveal?
—Where is the pain and destruction in this world?
—What gets our attention that something is amiss?
—What response is called for?

—What brings justice and relief?

—Where and what is God in this reflection?

—Where can we find grace and redemption in this reflection?

Step 7. Identify what you have learned. What are the challenges that this topic evokes for you?

Step 8. What thoughts and feelings now occur to you regarding the position you assumed at the beginning of this reflection?

Reflecting on Global Matters

Our universe is vast so a reflection that begins from something in the universe can be so global that we are truly unable to discern the trees in the forest. For that reason the starting point needs to be pinpointed. First there is the area to be considered. For instance, politics, the marketplace, science, or the arts may all offer interesting topics. And if we move to one of them, then a further selection needs to be made. If it is from the marketplace, then perhaps advertising will be a place to begin. Even then it will be necessary to select a particular advertisement (if in print) or a vignette from an advertisement if it is audio-visual. In other words, an artifact or specific item to initiate the reflection needs to be selected by a volunteer in the group or by group consensus.

While narrowing the focus for a reflection may seem too narrow, it will permit the group to focus in a meaningful way. If the topic is too large and the discussion lacks focus, then the conclusions of the reflection will be easily avoided. In other words, we are following the notion that a wall is erected one brick at a time. In the same way, a person's theology develops one reflection at a time, so that it eventually becomes a matrix.

Reflecting on a Cultural Text

In this context the word "text" is used in its broadest sense, so that it is not restricted to the written word. Any artifact of significance, or even a symbol of an artifact, might serve as a text that could generate a reflection. Thus a television program, a work of art, an advertisement, even a plant or an implement could be used as a basis. The requirement is that, whatever is used, it be an item that generates interest and energy for those involved in the seminar. Remember that the purpose of theological reflection is not to serve as a critique of culture, but to be a venue for developing the theology of those participating in the reflection.

EXTERIOR AND PUBLIC

Step 1. Select a text on which to focus. Identify the important characteristics, turning points, or salient characteristics of the text. Settle on one aspect to be pursued as the core of the reflection.

Step 2. At this point a decision needs to be made as to whether to pursue the reflection by developing a metaphor (alternative "a") that expresses the salient characteristics (See Appendix 1) or an issue statement (see Appendix 5), which is alternative "b."

ALTERNATIVE "A"

Explore the metaphor using the theological interrogatory of Chapter 13 as a guide.

ALTERNATIVE "B"

Develop an issue, explore the dimensions of the issue, and in the gap between the dimensions ask questions derived from the theological interrogatory of Chapter 13.

Step 3. Brainstorm what the tradition may say to the metaphor or issue that the group has developed. Select one item upon which to focus. If it is a written text, you may wish to read it, possibly from more than one translation if the text is biblical. Pose the same theological questions as were posed in the previous step.

INTERIOR AND PERSONAL

Step 4. Each member of the group now has an opportunity to share what her or his personal involvement might be with the issue or metaphor under review. A good question to pose is: What has happened in your life that reflects the same dynamics that are found in the metaphor or issue?

Step 5. What do you think or believe about what the group has discussed? What position might you take in regard to this if that became necessary?

Step 6. Insights and implications. This is an opportunity to identify and share what you have discovered and what it means for you in the future. What will you do with what you have learned? What does it imply for your life in the short or long term?

A Two-Valued Orientation
to Reflection

Much of our world is described by binary relationships. We have two hands, two eyes, and two feet. The basics for computers is binary, and each bit is either on or off. Binary relationships are a useful way to pinpoint a relationship so that it can be clearly identified. That also holds true when we try to reflect on complex ideas or decisions. This reflection introduces a binary approach to theological reflection, one based on a technical usage of the term "issue."[1] An issue can be something to debate or a problem faced by an individual or society. That understanding, however, is not sufficient for the purpose of theological reflection. An "issue" as defined for this purpose is a paradoxical statement. Both sides of the paradox are equally attractive and applicable. They represent a tension in which we live that is inescapable. The question is: How do we live productively within the tension we experience? Some examples are:

"I love to travel with my work, but/and I love to be at home with my family."

"I have a wonderful job opportunity in a faraway place that will have many benefits for me and my family, but/and I have responsibilities for my elderly parents and am called to remain where I live to care for them."

1. An issue-centered analysis of theological questions emerged from the work done by the Educational Center, St. Louis, Missouri. This method has been widely used by Christian educators since the 1960s. It was adapted by the Education for Ministry program as one of its recommended methods of theological reflection in 1977 and was subsequently modified numerous times. This presentation is a modified version based on the work of the Educational Center and the Education for Ministry program.

Almost every decision we make that has tension in it can be expressed by an "issue statement." Doing so can be very helpful to clarify the factors in a decision by taking the next step, examining the two dimensions of the issue by writing down in two columns under each clause what the cost and the promise of each dimension may be.[2] To pursue one of the examples above:

I love to travel with my work.

Cost:

I am away from home a lot.

My family relationships suffer.

I become very fatigued with the travel.

Promise:

My income is better.

I get a zest from meeting people.

I visit a lot of interesting places.

I am stimulated and energized by the travel.

I love to be home with my family.

Cost:

Loss of income.

I lose the sharpness that comes with being in touch.

I may miss out on promotions.

Promise:

I can enjoy the company and support of my family.

I have time to relax and enjoy life.

I can be with the people I love the most.

The Gap

The conjunctions *but/and*, which connect the two independent clauses of the issue statement, represent a gap between the two dimensions of the issue that is selected. That gap can be a very fruitful place to examine the theological aspects of the issues we face. By leaving a space between the columns one can note under that issue (within the gap of the two dimensions) what the world looks like (creation), what is destructive (sin), what brings it to attention (judgment), what is called for

2. Another way to tease out the dimensions of an issue is to ask what the risks and benefits of a particular decision are.

(repentance), and what brings celebration (redemption). One can also ask who God is in this tension or gap, which is a part of our lives.

Developing an Issue Statement

An issue statement must meet certain criteria to qualify as a useful statement for reflection. These are:

It must be universal.
It must be personal.
It must be balanced.
It must be true to life.

It should be articulated in two positive statements (not antithetical) that are obvious and possible choices.

Procedure for Reflection with an Issue Statement

Step 1. A volunteer offers an event of her or his life as a point from which to begin the reflection. Please note how Step 1 is to be done in Appendix 1 (p.188).

Step 2. Identify the key turning points or moments of energy in the event. Select one on which to focus.

Step 3. Identify the thoughts and feelings that were present at the point that was selected for reflection.

Step 4. Other participants "buy in" by identifying events from their lives that contained a similar coterie of thoughts and feelings.

Step 5. Brainstorm issue statements that express the paradox or tension of the point that was selected for reflection. It may be possible to develop an issue statement by mixing and matching the clauses until a statement is produced that the group can agree to pursue.

Step 6. Examine the cost and the promise (or risk and benefit) of each statement.

Step 7. Apply the theological interrogatory and ask the theological questions. (Note: This step may be omitted if the group prefers to restrict the reflection to questions applying to moral and ethical concerns.)

Step 8. Examine the tradition by brainstorming passages from the Christian tradition that seem to apply to the issue under scrutiny. Select one to pursue. If Step 7 was omitted, find the issue in the passage and analyze the issue. If Step 7 was included, then ask the theological questions. This decision is needed so that when comparisons are made the group is comparing similar information.

Step 9. This is a time for informal conversation around what has been done so far. It is an opportunity to compare and contrast the various sources. What seems to agree and where do differences exist? If insights emerge, be sure to note them.

Step 10. Bring in the exterior world. What is the cultural dimension of the issue? It may help to restrict the group to a particular area of culture.

Step 11. Now is the time to examine what different people believe about the issue, about the Scriptures that were reviewed, about the cultural implications, and about how all these relate.

Step 12. Now comes a time to gather the insights and implications that have emerged. What have we learned? What are we going to do with what we have learned? Who else may be involved in our decisions?

Reflection and Multiple Values

At the 1998 Lambeth Conference of Bishops, Rowan Williams, bishop of Monmouth, Wales, who was to become the next archbishop of Canterbury,[1] addressed the Anglican bishops from throughout the world at a plenary session on making moral decisions. He began:

> What is it like to make a choice? The temptation we easily give way to is to think that it's always the same kind of thing or that there's one kind of decision-making that's serious and authentic, and all other kinds ought to be like this. In our modern climate, the tendency is to imagine that choices are made by something called the individual will, faced with a series of clear alternatives, as if we were standing in front of the supermarket shelf. There may still be disagreement about what the "right" choice would be, but we'd know what making the choice was all about.

The archbishop went on to point out to the conference that we do not always know with clarity the best, much less the "right," course to follow or the "right" choice to make.

Appendix 5 presents a reflection that uses an analytical basis that is two-valued. When there are only two options or two values to consider, the choice is easier, and the reflection has the advantage of clarity. Its disadvantage is that two-valued orientations inevitably are much simpler than life. While it may seem that we are always between two options, in actuality every decision leaves us only on one path, while many other possibilities are disregarded. The question with this method, therefore, is how we are to proceed with a reflection that takes into consideration more than two values or considers more than two options.

1. The archbishop of Canterbury is the titular head of the Anglican Communion.

An example of the predicament we actually face in life is to expand the example offered in Appendix 5. It presented an issue in terms of my desire to travel and perform effectively in my profession and the desire to spend quality time with my family. I could not do both simultaneously. In reality, however, there are other pressures. I desire to spend time with my colleagues. I want to spend time improving my skills and developing new ones. I want to spend time with my favorite hobby. I want to meet the demands of elderly parents who need attention. I want some time to myself to relax and meditate. I want time to worship or go on a retreat. I need time to attend to my physical condition, exercise, undergo a physical, have my eyes checked, and let the dentist look over my teeth. None of these can be done simultaneously. All are valid, although some may take precedence and some may be neglected. In reality, when I consider a business trip, any number of these values in my life may affect my decision to go, for how long, when to leave and return, and other activities may be rescheduled accordingly. When reviewing my theological assumptions, the values of each aspect of my decision reflects my theological position and the dilemma that is posed in the world in which I live, the doctrine of creation that surrounds my life. This method of reflection attempts to give consideration in the reflection process to the multiple values and demands that form the realities of our lives.

A Multi-Valued Reflection

Step 1. Start by selecting from one of these three areas of the four-source model and identify material in that area with which you desire to work.

a) Share an event from your personal life from which you would like to learn. After the group hears the story, work together to identify at least four different ways to interpret that event. Take your thoughts and feelings into account as you develop this.

or

b) Take an event from culture (politics, business, law, medicine, education, art, music) and identify at least four different ways or perspectives by which to interpret the event.

or

c) Take a passage or event from the Bible or Church tradition and express the different points of view within the event. (i.e., Take the story of the Flood in Genesis. What are the points of view of God, of Noah, of his family, of those left behind, of those saved, of the animals?)

Step 2. Generate an image or metaphor. An image can be very rich and can encompass many aspects of an experience. Draw an image that encompasses all the different desires, values, or interpretations.

Step 3. EXPLORE THE WORLD OF THE IMAGE OR METAPHOR.

a) What kind of world does this image describe?
b) Where do you find evil and destruction in this image?
c) Where do you find faith in this image?
d) Where do you find grace in this image?
e) What kind of God(s) dwell in this image?

Step 3 (alternate). Apply a multi-valued orientation to an issue statement. For many issues there may be at least four or more perspectives to examine. For instance, you may have a job offer. An obvious issue you may face at some time or another is:

> I want to stay in my present job where I love the work
> and
> I want to take on the challenge of a new job.

But there are really more than two issues here:

> I want to stay in my job.
> I want to do what I love doing.
> I want opportunities to try new challenges.
> I want opportunities to go to new places.

Step 4. Explore the tradition (omit this step if you began with a passage from tradition).

a) Identify passages or events in our Christian tradition that speak to the image you have been exploring.
b) Select one passage or event and ask questions from the theological interrogatory.

Step 5. Explore what you understand our culture says (omit this step if you began with an event that emerges from our culture).

a) Identify a particular event from culture with which you wish to work. It needs to be something everyone knows about, although there may be very different perspectives between group members.

b) Ask questions from the theological interrogatory.

Step 6. Compare and contrast.

Where are there differences?
Where does agreement exist?

Step 7. BRING IN THE POSITION SOURCE.

a) What is your personal belief about this issue?
b) What are you willing to uphold as your fundamental point of view?

Step 8. Identify what you have learned.

What new thoughts or ideas cross your mind as a result of this reflection?
What feelings does this reflection evoke for you?

Step 9. Decide on the implications.

What must/should you do as a result of what you have learned? (Deciding to do nothing is a decision that is just as valid as a decision to act.)
What do you wish to do? Is there a dilemma for you?

Step 10. What does this mean for others?

What resources do you need to act on your decision?
What steps can you take to support this decision?
In what way might your action affect others around you, in your community, in the larger world?

Reflection with Movement

The reflection methods in the first six Appendices are sedentary processes. Usually people would pursue them sitting comfortably in a circle or perhaps around a large table. Some people, however, learn better with movement. This method was adapted from a method produced for the Education for Ministry program by Angela Hock and Richard Brewer. It allows participants to be physically active while engaging in a reflection process. The key to the process is to be thoroughly aware of the sources for the reflection.

There are five key physical locations that must be identified for the reflection. Four locations, located at cardinal points in the corner of a large area, are the four sources for a reflection. The fifth locus is the center of the room or space to be used. The area needs to be large enough to allow freedom for moving. It can be done with large groups, and of course the larger the group, the more space will be required.

Any of the methods described in the other Appendices may be followed. Some newsprint may be hung on a wall where it is visible to all so that the process of reflection may be tracked. The key to this process is that participants must physically locate themselves at the point established as the locus for a particular source. In other words, if someone is telling their story, that person will do so from the position in the room allocated to action. If someone is offering a passage of Scripture, that person will move to the area allocated for the tradition. When unsure, the participant should move to the center of the room. The group may help decide where that person should be after listening to the information that is offered.

Reflection with Large Groups—
The Fishbowl

The reflection methods outlined thus far are intended for used in groups that are relatively small, not more than twelve persons. Several factors militate against using these methods with larger groups. The most important are that the group is too large to develop trust, the time is insufficient to permit full participation by all present, and the number of voices will so diffuse the conversation that it will lose all momentum. Instead of a conversation, a series of monologues will result.

Appendices 8 and 9 offer two ways to introduce these reflection processes to large groups. The first is the fishbowl, which is appropriate for groups that have between twelve and thirty-five participants. The second is multiple tables, which is useful for very large groups. Any of the methods outlined in earlier Appendices may be used with large groups. Obviously, however, the intimacy will be lacking. Nevertheless, such reflections can be useful to a community working through difficult decisions or seeking to develop a basis for reconciliation through a better understanding of itself and the points of view of its members

Fishbowl

Any of the methods outlined in earlier Appendices may be used. The fishbowl is an especially helpful way to engender discussion among academics, who tend to be more formal and stylized in their approach to participating in a seminar.

Step 1. Organize the central space for a group of not more than twelve persons sitting in a circle. Invite some of the participants who will be in the reflection to fill ten of those chairs. Leave two chairs vacant as part of the central core. Other participants will sit in a larger circle around the inner circle. Everyone should be able to see the board or easel on which newsprint will be used to track the reflection.

Step 2. Advise those outside the group that if they wish to join the discussion, they may fill one of the vacant chairs and speak. Once done, they are to leave the conversation so that others may have an opportunity to fill the chair. On some occasions, participants among the original ten may feel done and leave the core group, in which case others may be free to move into the vacant chairs.

Step 3. Proceed with the reflection. Obviously, if the group does not know the steps, the guidance or mentoring will need to be fairly explicit.

Note: It is important to keep the process moving so that interest and energy will not lag.

Step 4. When the reflection is completed, ask the core cluster to remain quiet while those who remained outside have an opportunity to say what they believe and also to articulate what they have learned.

Step 5. Allow the conversation to flow between the core group and those on the outside.

Step 6. Ask everyone, but first the outer group, what they have learned that they will take away from this exercise.

Step 7. This step is necessary only if you are using this as a demonstration/method to teach others the process. If so, then take time to debrief the group about the method.

Reflection with Large Groups— Multiple Tables

It is possible to teach theological reflections to large groups, probably up to 250 persons. Of course, a large space is required, and a sound system that will carry throughout the chamber must be used, along with microphones spotted at key locations accessible to participants.

Use any of the reflection methods described in the previous Appendices. If the reflection is to begin with someone's life experience, then the guide or mentor needs to be sure that this person will be able to relate his or her story in a concise manner.

The participants should be arranged around tables or in circles of six to ten persons. As each step unfolds, the discussion is to take place within the small group. If the group is less than a hundred (approximately ten or fewer subgroups in circles or at tables), the guide may ask for brief reports about the activity at each table as the reflection proceeds. That will not be possible if the group is larger. In that case the guide will lead the entire group through the exercise on a precise time schedule that gives each subgroup time for discussion but then ends on a signal from the leader so that the next step can be pursued.

At the end it is important to allow fifteen to twenty minutes for significant insights to be shared with the entire community as well as to explore with everyone the process that was followed.

APPENDIX 10

Theological Reflection
A Quick Introduction

It is possible to introduce theological reflections to groups of various sizes in a traditional setting rather than in the confines of a seminar. This exercise can be done in about half an hour to forty-five minutes.

Step 1. Prepare a large surface that can be viewed by everyone by drawing a mandela (a circle with four spokes—see the chart on p. 190). To the side, post or reserve an area and label it "insights." In the mandela label the four quadrants with the four sources.

Step 2. Select an object or event known to everyone from which to begin the reflection. I have used the following stock examples:

a) From tradition—the Bible
b) From experience—I arrived too late to catch my flight.
c) From the world around us—a panhandler asks for money.

Step 3. Draw an image of the experience in the center of the mandela.

Step 4. Obtain a general commitment that the core of the reflection is an experience everyone has shared. If not, try another idea on which to focus and place it in the center of the mandela.

Step 5. Depending upon the image selected, use the quadrant from which it is drawn and write in the group's off-the-cuff responses to:

Look at this image. What does the world of this image look like? What does it feel like? What goes wrong with this world? What would make it right?

Step 6. Ask people to respond at random to each of the remaining quadrants in the mandela. Quickly write in the responses. Some questions to ask are:

Action or behavior: What has happened to you in relationship to . . .
Tradition: What does our Christian tradition say to . . .
Culture: What does the world around us say about . . .
Belief: What do you think of what we have gathered so far?

Step 7. Ask for what has been learned and put these on the paper prepared for insights. Have you had any "Aha" moments today with this reflection? What might you think about differently as a result of our time together?

Note: It is important to keep the flow moving, to write quickly, and to maintain energy. Just let those who are moved to speak do so. This is a process geared to engage the extroverts more than the introverts, so it may be helpful at times to stop and ask for a short silence to reflect on the next step. Doing so will allow those who need time to ponder their offering the space in which to prepare what they wish to say.

Bibliography

Adler, Mortimer J. *The Paideia Proposal: An Educational Manifesto.*
New York: Macmillan, 1982.
_____. *The Paideia Program.* New York: Macmillan, 1984.
Bailie, Gil. *Violence Unveiled.* New York: Crossroad, 1995.
Booty, John E. *What Makes Us Episcopalians?* Wilton, Conn.: Morehouse-
Barlow, 1982.
Campbell, Joseph. *The Masks of God: Creative Mythology.* New York:
Penguin Books, rpt. 1978.
Cano, Melchior. *De locis theologicis libri duodecim.* Salamanca, 1563.
Cited in Raymond F. Collins. *Models of Theological Reflection.*
Boston: University Press of America, 1984.
Clarke, Gerald. "The Need for New Myths." *Time* (January 17, 1972).
Clebsch, William A., and Charles R. Jaekle. *Pastoral Care in Historical
Perspective.* Northvale, N.J.: Jason Aronson, 1994.
Collins, Raymond F. *Models of Theological Reflection.* Boston: Univer-
sity Press of America, 1984.
Erikson, Erik. *Identity, Youth, and Crisis.* New York: W.W. Norton,
1968.
Farley, Edward. *Theologia: The Fragmentation and Unity of Theological
Education.* Philadelphia: Fortress Press, 1983.
Farrar, Austin M. *The Glass of Vision.* London: Dacre Press, 1948.
Fowler, James W. *Becoming Adult, Becoming Christian: Adult Develop-
ment and Christian Faith.* Rev. ed. San Francisco: Jossey-Bass Pub-
lishers, 2000.
Friedrichs, Robert W. *A Sociology of Sociology.* New York: The Free
Press, 1970.
Girard, René. *Violence and the Sacred.* Trans. Patrick Gregory. Balti-
more: Johns Hopkins University Press, 1979.

Gregorc, Anthony F. *Gregorc Style Delineator: A Self-Assessment Instrument for Adults.* Columbia, Conn.: Gregorc Associates, Inc., 1985.

Griffis, James. "The Dialectic of Experience." Unpublished paper presented to the Conference of Anglican Theologians. West Cornwall, Conn., September 22, 1994.

Hout, Michael, and Claude S. Fischer. "Losing Religion, but Not Spirituality." *American Sociological Review* (April 2002).

Killen, Patricia O'Connell, and John de Beer. *The Art of Theological Reflection.* New York: Crossroad, 1994.

_____. "Everyday Theology: A Model for Religious and Theological Education." *Chicago Studies.* Vol. 22, no. 2 (August 1983).

Kuhn, Thomas S. *The Structure of Scientific Revolutions.* Also issued as *International Encyclopedia of Unified Science.* Vol. 2, no. 2. Ed. Otto Neurath. Chicago: University of Chicago Press, 1970.

Lonergan, Bernard J. F. *Method in Theology.* New York: Seabury Press, 1972.

Malinowski, Bronislaw. "Culture." In *Encyclopedia of Social Sciences,* 4:621ff.

Mascall, Eric L. *Christian Theology and Natural Science.* London: Longmans Green and Co., 1956.

Naisbitt, John. *Megatrends: Ten New Directions Transforming Our Lives.* New York: Warner Books, 1982.

Niebuhr, H. Richard. *Christ and Culture.* New York: Harper & Row, 1951.

Ogletree, Thomas W. *The Death of God Controversy.* Nashville: Abingdon Press, 1966.

Rahner, Karl, ed. *Encyclopedia of Theology.* New York: Seabury Press, 1975.

_____. "Reflections on Methodology and Theology." In *Confrontations I.* Vol. 11 of *Theological Investigations.* New York: Seabury Press, 68–164, 1974.

Richardson, Alan. "The Rise of Modern Biblical Scholarship and Recent Discussion of the Authority of the Bible." *The Cambridge History of the Bible.* Ed. S. L. Greensdale. Cambridge: The University Press, rpt. 1976.

Rogers, Carl R. *Freedom to Learn.* Columbus, Ohio: Charles E. Merrill, 1969.

Schillebeeckx, Edward. *Geloofsverstaan: Interpretatie en Krietiek.* Bloemendaal: Nelissen, 1972.

Toffler, Alvin. *Future Shock*. New York: Random House, 1970.

_____. *Power Shift: Knowledge, Wealth, and Violence at the Edge of of 21st Century*. New York: Bantam Books, 1990.

Tolkien, J.R.R. *The Hobbit, or, There and Back Again*. London: Allen & Unwin, 1984, 1976.

Torrance, Thomas F. *Theological Science*. London: Oxford University Press, 1969.

Tracy, David. *Blessed Rage for Order: The New Pluralism in Theology*. New York: Seabury Press, 1978.

Ward, Ted. "Programmed Learning Technique Workshop." In *Theological Education by Extension*. Ed. Ralph D. Winter, 321–322. South Pasadena, Calif.: William Carey Press, 1969.

Whaling, Frank. "The Development of the Word 'Theology.'" *Scottish Journal of Theology* 34 (1981) 289–312.

Wheatley, Margaret J. *Leadership and the New Science*. San Francisco: Berrett Koehlers, 1992.

Wheelwright, Philip. *Metaphor and Reality*. 2nd ed. Bloomington, Ind.: Midland Books, 1968.

Whitehead, James D., and Evelyn Eaton Whitehead. *Method in Ministry: Theological Reflection and Christian Ministry*. San Francisco: Harper & Row, 1980.

Whitrow, G. J. *The Structure of the Universe*. London: Hutchinson, 1946.

Index

217